YOUR FIRST 10
ACOUSTIC GUITAR LESSONS

CHRISTIAN & AMY JOY TRIOLA

An imprint of
Tenterhook Books, LLC
Akron, Ohio

Discover what you've been missing.

Copyright ©2023, 2022 Christian J. Triola, Amy Joy Triola

All Rights Reserved.

Except as permitted under the U.S. Copyright Act of 1976, no part of this publication may be reproduced, distributed, or transmitted, in whole or in part, in any form or by any means, or stored in any form of retrieval system, without prior written consent of the author.

Bulk sales inquiries can be directed to the author at info@themissingmethod.com.

Cover and Book Design by Amy Joy, ©2022 Amy Joy

The Missing Method™ for Guitar is an imprint of Tenterhook Books, LLC. The Missing Method name and logos are property of Tenterhook Books, LLC.

ISBN-13: 978-1953101228 (paperback)

CONTENTS

Introduction 1

LESSON 1: The Basics and Your First Chords 2

   1.1 Get Acquainted with Your Guitar 2
       1.11 How to Care for Your Guitar 4
       1.12 How to Tune Your Guitar 5
   1.2 Basic Technique 8
       1.21 How to Hold the Guitar 8
       1.22 How to Hold the Pick 10
       1.23 How to Strum the Guitar 11
       1.24 Fret Hand Technique 12
   1.3 Get Started with Chords 13
       1.31 How to Read a Chord Diagram 14
       1.32 Understanding Time 15
       1.33 A Quick Lesson in Music Theory 17
       1.34 Your First Chords 18
   1.4 How and What to Practice 19
   Day 1 Practice 19
   Day 2 Practice 20
   Day 3 Practice 20
   Day 4 Practice 21
   Day 5 Practice 21
   Day 6 Practice 22

LESSON 2: The Full Em, C, G, Am, & D Chords 23

   Day 1 Practice: The Full Em Chord 23
   Day 2 Practice: The Full G Chord 25
   Day 3 Practice: The Full C Chord 26
   Day 4 Practice: The Am Chord 28
   Day 5 Practice: The D Chord 29

Day 6 Practice: A Common Chord Progression 31

LESSON 3: A, D7, E, & B7 and Eighth Note Strumming 32
Day 1 Practice: The A Chord. 32
Day 2 Practice: The D7 Chord 34
Day 3 Practice: The E Chord 35
Day 4 Practice: The B7 Chord 37
Day 5 Practice: Eighth Note Strumming 39
Day 6 Practice: Combining Rhythms 41

LESSON 4: The Full F Chord & Chord Progressions. 43
Day 1 Practice: The F Major Chord. 43
Day 2 Practice: The Full F Major Chord 45
Day 3 Practice: Chord Progressions 47
Day 4 Practice: The Turnaround & The Repeat Sign 48
Day 5 Practice: Chord Progression 3 & Turnaround 2. 49
Day 6 Practice: Chord Progression 4, The 12-Bar Blues 50

LESSON 5: How to Read Tablature 52
Day 1 Practice: TAB for Familiar Tunes. 53
Day 2 Practice: Tablature for a full melody 54
Day 3 Practice: Riffs in TAB 55
Day 4 Practice: Two Note Tablature 56
Day 5 Practice: Chords in Tablature. 57
Day 6 Practice: Chords & TAB 58

LESSON 6: Building Technique with Warm-ups 59
Day 1 Practice: The Spider Walk. 59
Day 2 Practice: Spider Walk 2 61
Day 3 Practice: Spider Walk 3 62
Day 4 Practice: The Complete Spider Walk 63
Day 5 Practice: Alternate Picking The Spider Walk. 64
Day 6 Practice: Alternate Picking with Eighth Notes 65

LESSON 7: How to Read Standard Notation 66

The Elements of Reading Music 66
Day 1 Practice: Notes on the First String 68
Day 2 Practice: Melody on the First String 70
Day 3 Practice: Notes on the Second String 71
Day 4 Practice: Melodies on Two Strings 74
Day 5 Practice: Notes on the Third String 76
Day 6 Practice: Notes on All Three Strings 78

LESSON 8: Note Reading on Strings 4-6 80

More Elements of Reading Music 80
Day 1 Practice: Notes on the fourth string 81
Day 2 Practice: Notes on the 4th string without TAB 83
Day 3 Practice: Notes on the Fifth String 85
Day 4 Practice: Notes on Strings 1-5 88
Day 5 Practice: Notes on The Sixth String 90
Day 6 Practice: Notes on Strings 1-6 92

LESSON 9: Reading Accidentals 94

Day 1 Practice: Reading Sharps 94
Day 2 Practice: Reading Sharps, Part 2 96
Day 3 Practice: Reading Flats 97
Day 4 Practice: Reading Flats, Part 2 99
Day 5 Practice: Reading Naturals 100
Day 6 Practice: Key Signatures 101

LESSON 10: Fingerstyle Playing 103

Day 1 Practice: PIMA with E and G Major 105
Day 2 Practice: PIMA with C Major and A Minor 106
Day 3 Practice: PIMA with D Major and F Major 107
Day 4 Practice: PIMA-AMIP Pattern 110
Day 5 Practice: PIMIAIMI Pattern 111
Day 6 Practice: PM-PIPMPI Pattern 112

Songs for Practice **113**

   Chord Practice 113
   TAB Practice 114
   Note Reading Practice 115
   Fingerpicking Practice 116

Next Steps **118**

Further Resources **119**

Appendix **120**

   Chord reference 120
   How to Use a Capo 122
   Try it: Using a Capo 123
   How to Change Your Guitar Strings 124

About the Author **127**

INTRODUCTION

Welcome to Your First 10 Acoustic Guitar Lessons!

In the two decades I have taught guitar, one thing has become abundantly clear to me: students progress faster with clear, guided instruction and practice. Unfortunately, not everyone has the resources or opportunity to take private guitar lessons, and most method books have gaps in the curriculum that leave students scratching their heads and searching the internet for answers. And without private instruction (and sometimes with it), students often don't know what or how to practice.

With this in mind, my wife, Amy, and I set out to create a revolutionary new guitar method that would offer both the instruction you would get in private lessons as well as a guide as to what to practice so that anyone can learn to play guitar and see and hear themselves make progress faster.

That book you now hold in your hands, and we are incredibly excited to share it with you!

What you'll get from this book:
- Confidence: You can do this! You can play guitar!
- Ability: Follow these lessons and you will be playing guitar!
- Expertise: When you've finished, you'll be an acoustic guitar player, with the knowledge and experience to play hundreds of songs!

What you'll find inside:
- Step-by-step lessons including the same material as you would receive in private guitar lessons.
- Daily warm-up, practice, and review exercises.
- Specific guidance so you know how to warm-up, review, and what to practice each day.

Here's how it works:

For each of ten weeks, you'll find a new lesson focused on a particular skill. These are followed by six unique practice sessions, each designed to help you master that skill. These practices follow a three-fold system of Warm-up, Learn New, and Review. On day seven, you can review anything you like or give yourself a day off. As you follow this method, you'll quickly see and hear yourself making progress day by day, increasing your motivation to keep going!

Once you've completed *Your First 10 Acoustic Guitar Lessons*, you'll have the knowledge you need to play a whole lot of guitar music as well as a foundation you can build on to your heart's content.

So let's get started!

LESSON 1

THE BASICS AND YOUR FIRST CHORDS

Welcome to your first acoustic guitar lesson! In this lesson we'll cover a lot of ground, starting from the basics. But don't worry; by the end, we'll have you playing your first chords!

In this lesson, you will learn:

1. About your guitar, including the parts of the guitar and how to care for it.
2. How to tune your guitar.
3. How to hold the guitar
4. How to hold a pick and proper strumming technique.
5. Proper fretting hand technique.
6. How to read a chord diagram.
7. How to keep time.
8. How to strum your first three chords.
9. How to practice.

1.1 GET ACQUAINTED WITH YOUR GUITAR

Before we dive into playing, it's best to familiarize yourself with the instrument and some of the terminology.

The acoustic guitar is a stringed instrument that relies on a resonating chamber to produce the sound. This means that typically, the larger the resonating chamber, the larger the sound. Acoustic guitars can vary in size both in the length and width of the resonating chamber (the main box of the guitar), as well as in its depth.

While a large resonating chamber may produce a fairly large sound, if you are performing live, this may not be enough sound for the venue. For this reason, some acoustic guitars are equipped with the electronics to connect to an amplifier. This also provides the added benefit that the guitar can then be hooked up to sound processing pedals as well, to adjust the sound in various ways. This said, pedals and amplification are beyond the scope of your first ten lessons, so let's move on.

The neck of the guitar (see diagram below) can also come in different lengths and widths, depending on the size of the guitar, and this is something else to consider when choosing a guitar. Smaller frame adults and children will usually find they are more comfortable with a smaller scale guitar, with and a shorter, narrower neck for the fretting hand to more easily grab notes and chords.

The distance of the strings from the fretboard is called the **action**, and it will vary by guitar. Again, this is something to consider when choosing an instrument, as the lower the action, the easier it is on the fingers to hold notes and chords. The higher the action, the harder you will have to press down on the string to avoid string buzz (i.e.: the buzzing sound you'll hear if a string isn't pressed firmly when you play a note or chord). Also, the higher the action, the more likely it is that your fingers will become sore faster, especially when you are first starting out. For this reason, it's recommended to find an instrument with reasonably low action. If you aren't sure, ask for assistance at your local guitar shop as they should be able to steer you in the right direction.

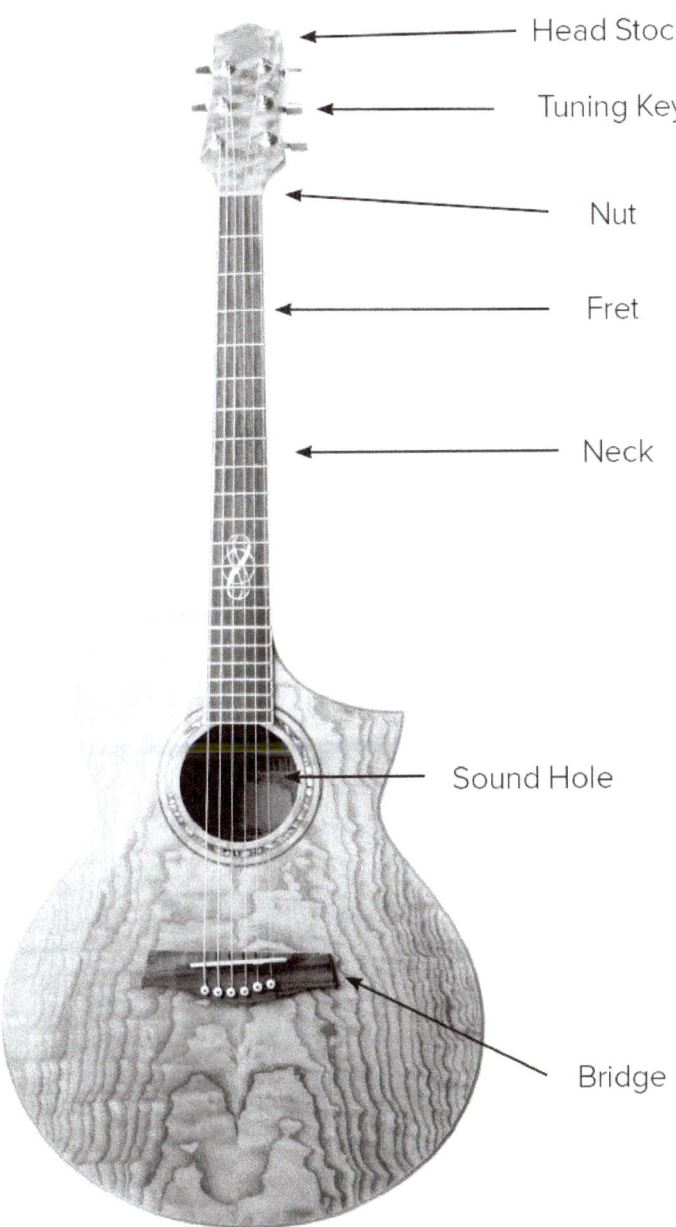

The guitar is a fretted instrument, which makes it easier to play than other stringed instruments. The frets make it easy to see where your notes are (the notes correspond to particular frets) and when the string is pressed, the fret stops the sound, helping you get a nice, clean sound. Many fretboards also include indicator dots, either on the fretboard itself or along the side of the fretboard so you can see them when you are playing. These are there to help you easily navigate the guitar neck, as they are located at the 5th, 7th, 9th, and 12th frets.

The top of the guitar is referred it as the **headstock**, and it is here that you will find the **tuning pegs**, or **tuners**. At the base of the guitar, below the **sound hole**, you will find the **bridge**. The strings attach from the tuners, over the nut at the top of the neck, and over the **saddle** on the bridge, and on most acoustic guitars, into pin holes at the base of the bridge. Bridge pins are placed in the pin holes to keep the strings in place. This system makes it fairly easy to change strings and get them in tune.

1.11 How to Care for Your Guitar

Taking care of your acoustic guitar involves more than just keeping in tune and the dust off. Here are 8 things to keep in mind to keep your guitar in great shape.

Tips for caring for your guitar:

1. Change the strings every one to six months, depending on how often you play. The more you play, the more often you'll want to change your strings.

2. Always use the same gauge (size) strings, unless you want to adjust your neck and try and something new.

3. Keep your guitar out of the sun. The heat can melt glue and warp wood.

4. Keep your guitar out of the cold. Cold weather shrinks the wood causing tuning and other intonation problems.

5. Consider getting a humidifier for your guitar, especially if you live in a dry climate or if the place where you store you guitar is particularly dry. The humidifier will keep the wood from drying and cracking and avoid potentially costly damage.

6. When you aren't playing it, keep your guitar away from vents and open windows. If possible, keep the guitar in its case in a place that maintains a constant temperature. Most guitars like it at about 76F degrees (24C).

7. Keep your guitar clean. However, do not use anything that can scratch the finish. A soft cloth or microfiber cloth should be used. To clean it, there guitar cleaners and polishes available that are made specifically for the guitar.

8. About once a year, be sure to clean and oil your fretboard. You can get fretboard oil at just about any music store.

1.12 How to Tune Your Guitar

Being able to tune your guitar is a vital skill that every player needs to have. Having it in tune allows you to play with other musicians, and it helps you to develop your listening skills as a musician. Like playing the guitar, tuning also takes practice. So it may take you a while your first several tries, but once you get used to it, it won't take any time at all.

Step 1: Learn the String Names

The first thing you need to know in order to tune the guitar is what notes to tune to. The chart below shows you the names of the pitches of each string.

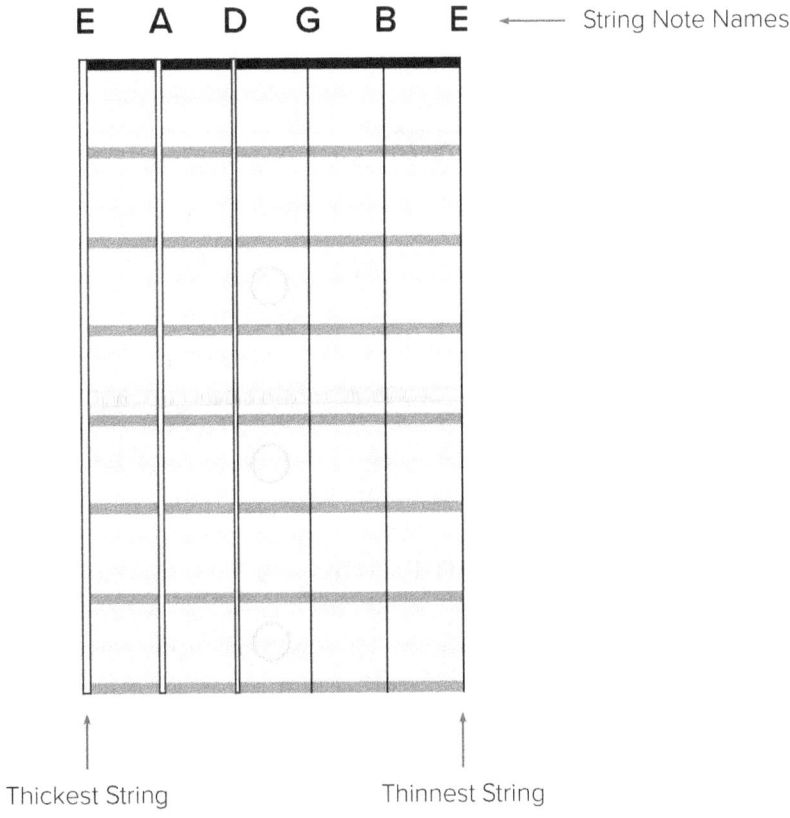

There are a couple of sayings that can help you remember the names of the strings, from thick to thin:

Eddie **A**te **D**ynamite, **G**ood **B**ye **E**ddie.

Or the less violent:

Every **A**mateur **D**oes **G**et **B**etter **E**ventually.

Step 2: Get your tuner ready

The easiest method for tuning a guitar is to use a tuner. Tuners come in all shapes and sizes. There are credit card sized tuners and clip-on tuners that attach to your guitar. There are lots of great apps available for Android and Apple devices as well, and many of these are free.

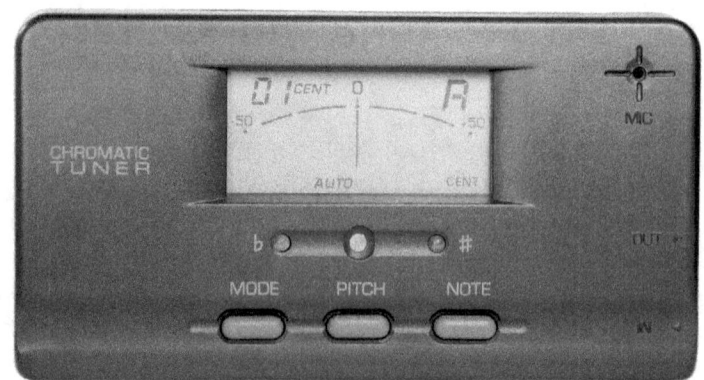

A typical credit card sized tuner

Another, but more challenging method for tuning is to use a reference pitch from an instrument that is already in tune. Most people use a piano, another in-tune guitar, or a pitch pipe to achieve this. In this case, you simply listen to the reference pitch and then match that pitch on your instrument. This can be difficult for beginners, but can help you to develop a strong ear as well as help you to develop your overall musicianship.

Step 3: Make Small Adjustments

Because changes in temperature and air quality can affect tuning, it is recommended that you check your tuning every time you play. This will also help you become accustomed to what an in-tune guitar sounds like.

That being said, once it's in tune, your guitar should stay fairly close to tune most of the time. Therefore, when you start tuning, be prepared to start with small adjustments, as that is often all that is needed.

Step 4: Tighten if low, loosen if high

The reason most people find a tuner easier to use than a reference pitch (see Step 2) is because most tuners will show which note you are playing and tell you whether the note is too low, too high, or in tune. Usually, a meter of some kind will display this information.

Working one string at a time, adjust the corresponding tuning key on the headstock.

    --> If the string is too **low**, you'll want to **tighten** the string.

    --> If the string is too **high**, you'll want to **loosen** it.

In addition to watching the screen of your tuner, be sure to listen to the sound of the string as well. Your ear will help you figure out if you are going too far from the in-tune note.

Step 5: Practice Tuning Often

Tuning can be a little intimidating or frustrating at first. This is another reason why practicing checking your tuning each time you pick up your guitar is a good idea. Like anything new, once you've done it a few times it gets easier and faster, until eventually it becomes second nature.

For more help with tuning, be sure to check out The Missing Method YouTube channel. There you will find video tutorials on how to tune your guitar as well as how to keep your guitar in tune. Find it at: https://bit.ly/Missing-Method-YouTube.

1.2 BASIC TECHNIQUE

Now that you know about your guitar and how to care for it, it's time to start playing! To do so, we first need to talk about some basic techniques. These are designed to make playing as easy and comfortable as possible, so practicing these as a new player will help cement good habits as you continue playing. That being said, everyone's body is different, so you may find you need to adapt to your own needs. It's recommended, however, that if possible, you try the techniques below first.

1.21 How to Hold the Guitar

There are three main ways you can hold your guitar.

METHOD 1:
Traditional Method

The first and most common method is to have the curved part of the guitar's body seated on your right leg. (See photo.)

For this method, keep your feet flat on the floor, your picking arm resting comfortably on top, and make sure your hand is just behind the sound hole. Also, for more stability, be sure to use a strap.

METHOD 2:
Classical Method

The second method is the classical guitar method, where you use a footstool or pillow to hold the guitar up on your left leg. (See photo at left.)

This method keeps the guitar neck at a greater angle, making it easier to access the entire fretboard.

METHOD 3:
Standing Method

The third method is to get a strap and stand with the guitar. This is best for performance, but it can be tiring when practicing. However, it can be beneficial to practice both seated and standing.

When standing, be careful not to place the strap too low, as this can hurt your technique and your posture. Instead, adjust it to a comfortable level so that it feels similar to how your play when seated. (See photo at right.)

1.22 How to Hold the Pick

1. First, curve the fingers of your picking hand inward. Keep them relaxed. Don't make a fist.

2. Next, place the pick on top of the first knuckle so that the point of the pick faces outward.

3. Finally, place your thumb over the pick to hold it in place. This may feel awkward or uncomfortable at first, but once you get used to it, you'll have full control over the pick.

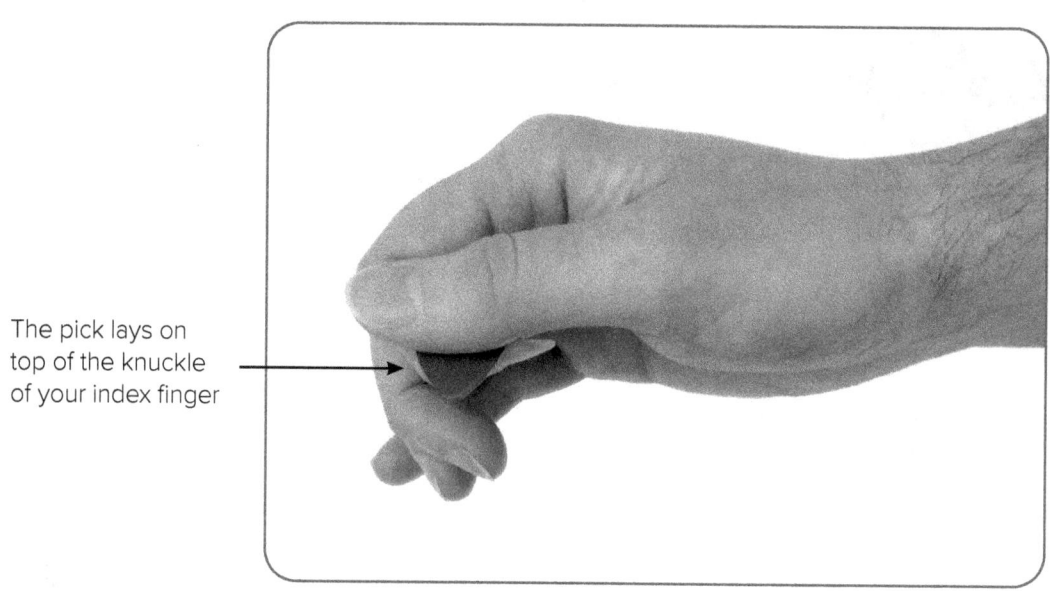

The pick lays on top of the knuckle of your index finger

When I'm not using it, I like to tuck my pick gently under my B string, near the nut of my guitar. It keeps it handy, and in 30 years, I haven't lost a pick yet!

1.23 How to Strum the Guitar

When strumming, don't use your whole arm; simply swing from the wrist. To do this, start with your wrist slightly bent upward, then release the pick across the strings in a natural semi-circular motion. Don't force it or overthink it. Just let your picking hand glide over the strings.

The wrist angles up slightly

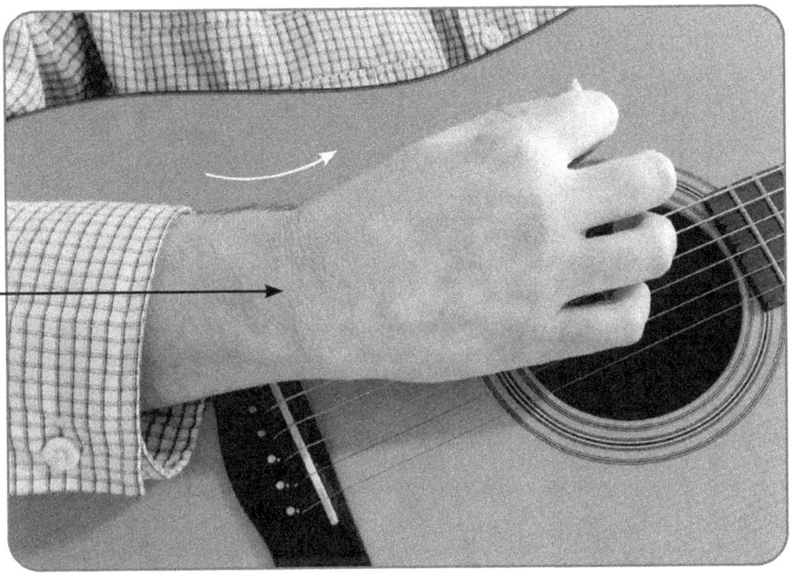

The arm stays in place, and the wrist moves

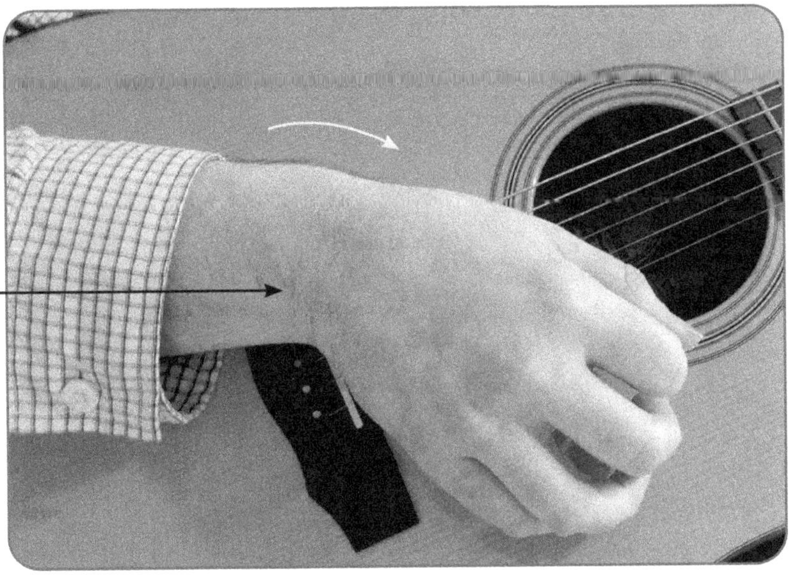

Tip:
It takes a while to develop control over this motion, but in time it will become second nature.

1.24 Fret Hand Technique

Proper fret hand technique is crucial in order to get a good sound and avoid injury.

1. First, always keep your fingers up on their tips. The fingers should be spread apart and not touch each other.

2. Second, when playing a single note, do not press against the fret itself, but rather press just behind the fret on the fretboard. Pressing too far behind the fret will result in buzzing, so you'll want to make sure you are consistently pressing down just behind the fret.

3. Third, the wrist should be dropped down and the thumb planted behind the neck so that the thumb lines up between the index and middle fingers when looking at it from above.

4. Fourth, the knuckles of your hand should be running completely parallel to the neck, and the palm of your hand should not make contact with the neck.

1.3 GET STARTED WITH CHORDS

Now that your guitar is in tune and you have an idea of how to position your hands on the guitar, we can start playing. There are several different approaches to learning the guitar when you are starting out. Many will learn to read notes first, while others learn chords. The acoustic guitar practically screams to be strummed, so in this book, we will be learning chords first.

A **chord** is any combination of 2 or more notes played at the same time (strummed). The most common chords consist of three notes and can be played in a variety of ways on the guitar.

To begin, you'll first want to understand how to read a chord chart. The diagram on the next page will help you do this.

1.31 How to Read a Chord Diagram

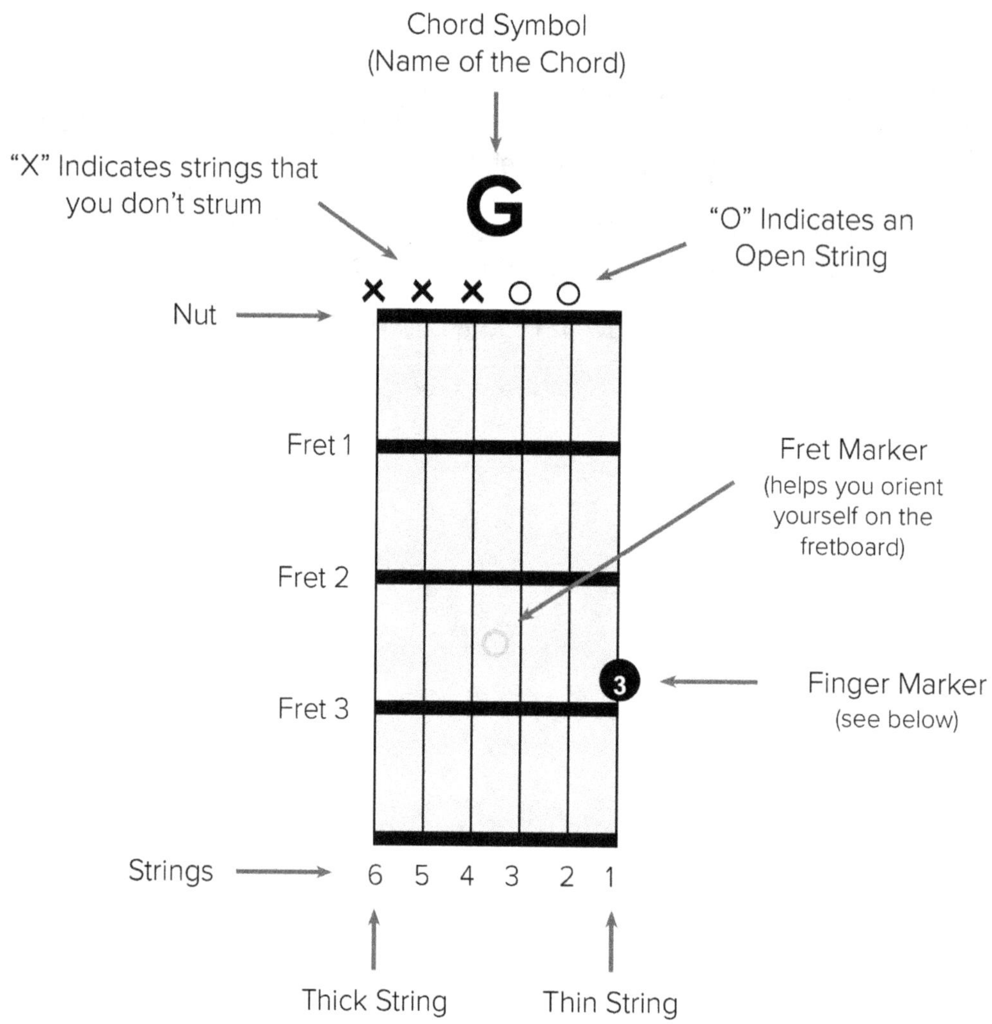

Chord Symbol
(Name of the Chord)

G

"X" Indicates strings that you don't strum

"O" Indicates an Open String

Nut

Fret 1

Fret 2

Fret Marker
(helps you orient yourself on the fretboard)

Fret 3

Finger Marker
(see below)

Strings → 6 5 4 3 2 1

Thick String   Thin String

The finger markers correspond to the fingers as numbered to the right

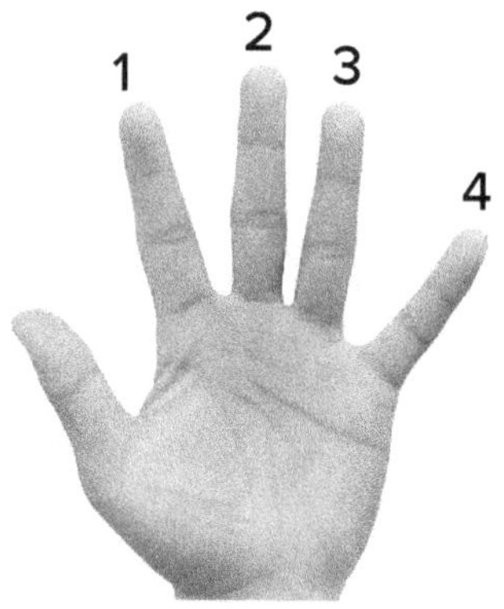

Technique Tip:

When placing fingers on the fretboard, always keep your wrist dropped and your fingers on their tips. Remember only your fingertips and the thumb behind the neck should be touching the guitar. Keep the palm of your hand off the neck. This will help you build finger strength and solid technique.

1.32 Understanding Time

Now that you know how read a chord chart, your next step is to understand how chords move through time. After strumming a chord, you have a choice to make: do you strum the same chord again? Do you move on to a different chord? Or do you let the chord ring out? To show these ideas on paper, **slash notation** is used. (See the example of slash notation the next page.) Slash notation is similar to standard musical notation, but instead of specific pitches being indicated, only rhythms are shown. That way you can figure out how to strum a song without having to read every single note present in each chord.

To understand how this works, we'll start with the **staff**. The staff contains five lines and four spaces with a **clef** at the beginning to indicate a set of **pitches** or range of sounds. Keep in mind, however, that with slash notation, these specific pitches aren't shown.

The clef used in guitar music (shown below) is called the **treble clef**, meaning that the sounds found in this staff are the midrange to higher pitches in music. The staff's second function is to help you keep track of time. This is done by dividing the staff into sections called **bars** or **measures**. In doing so, it makes reading slash notation easier by organizing it.

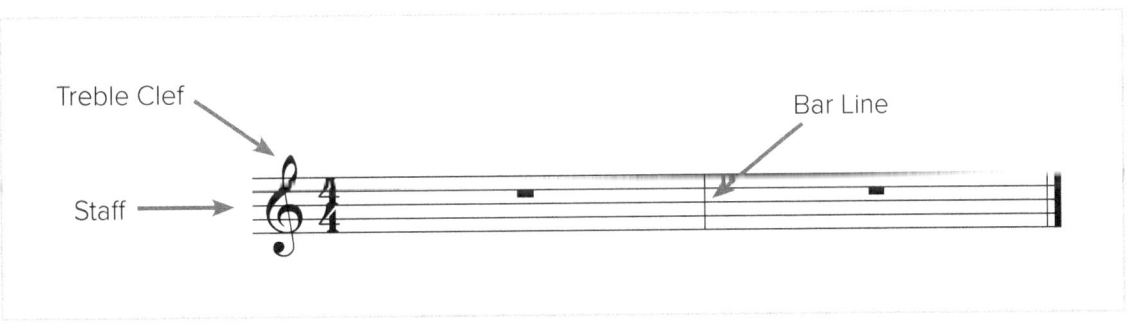

Each measure is only allowed a certain number of **beats**. This limitation allows us to keep track of time. The grouping of these beats is called **meter**. The most common meter is four beats per measure called **4/4 time**, as seen in the example below.

Beat is the underlying current of music. You don't necessarily hear the beat. Think of it as a second hand on a clock, a constant steady clicking that helps you keep track of time.

What you actually play is the **rhythm**. Rhythm tells you how long or how short a pitch or chord should be held. For example, in 4/4 time a **whole note** (see below) is sustained for four beats. A **half note** is sustained for two beats. A **quarter note** (which takes up a quarter of the measure) is sustained for only one beat.

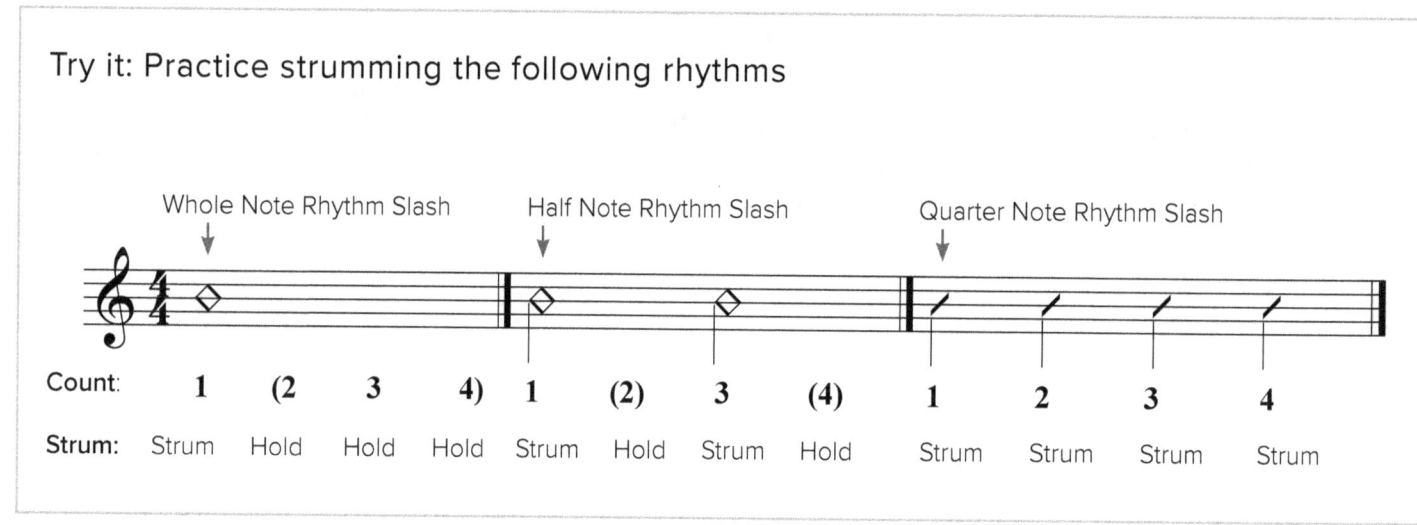

1.33 A Quick Lesson in Music Theory

Major, Minor, & Dominant Seventh Chords

In music, any combination of pitches is considered a **chord**, so there are as many chords as there are combinations of sounds. Despite this seemingly endless number of possible combinations, most of them boil down to three primary types: major, minor, and dominant seven.

These labels refer to the sound the chord makes. So you could say a **major chord** sounds major, a **minor chord** sounds minor, etc. When comparing the sounds of these chords, minor sounds lower and darker than major, and **dominant seven** sounds like a more unstable version of major. These three sounds are the basis for a countless number of songs.

Chord Symbols

The **chord symbol** is simply the name of the chord you are to strum placed above the measure. When a chord is major, it will be shown by a single letter name (for example: G). When a chord is minor, there will be a lowercase "m" next to the letter (example: Gm). The dominant seven chords will have the number seven next to them (example: G7).

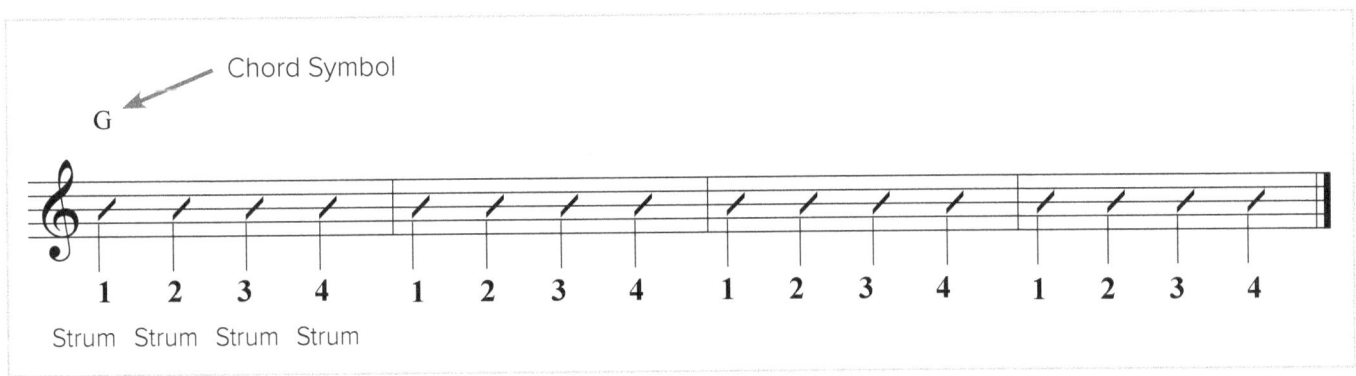

1.34 Your First Chords

Below you will find three simple chords to start with. Try each one of them using the rhythms indicated. Pay close attention to which strings are played and which are avoided, noted in each chord chart. Be sure not to rush, even if it seems easy to do. Keep your time steady and your chords as clear as you can get them.

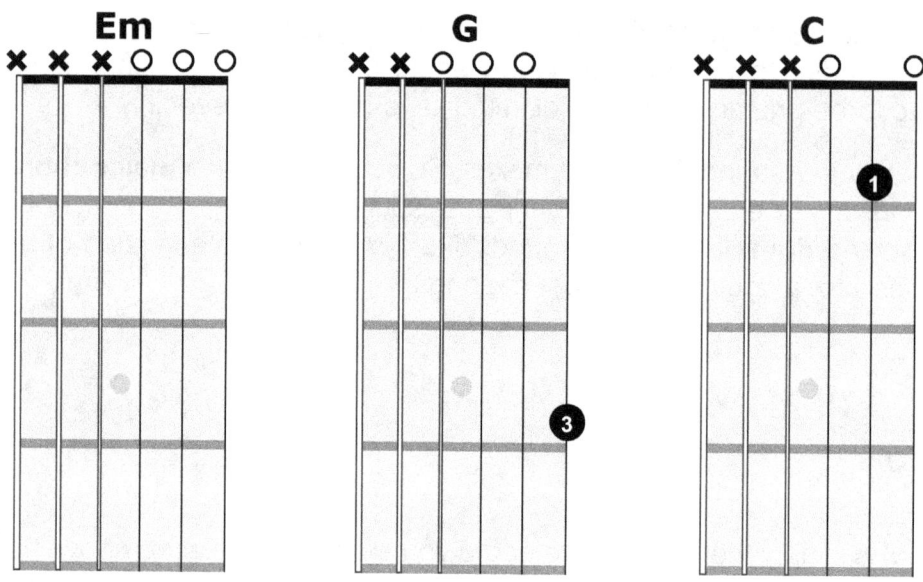

Try it: Practice strumming the following chords.

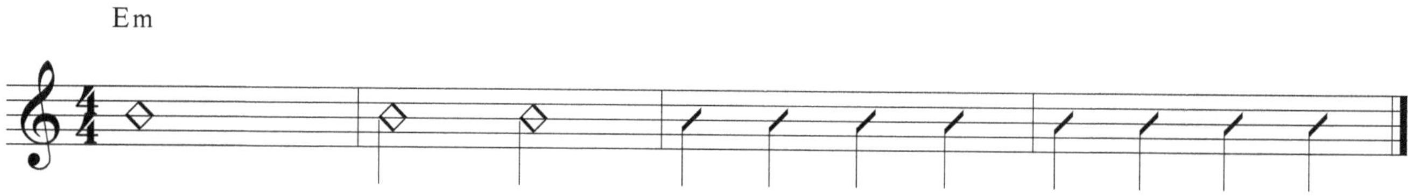

Em

Count: 1 (2 3 4) 1 (2) 3 (4) 1 2 3 4 1 2 3 4
Strum: Strum Hold Hold Hold Strum Hold Strum Hold Strum Strum Strum Strum Strum Strum Strum Strum

G

Count: 1 (2 3 4) 1 (2) 3 (4) 1 2 3 4 1 2 3 4
Strum: Strum Hold Hold Hold Strum Hold Strum Hold Strum Strum Strum Strum Strum Strum Strum Strum

C

Count: 1 (2 3 4) 1 (2) 3 (4) 1 2 3 4 1 2 3 4
Strum: Strum Hold Hold Hold Strum Hold Strum Hold Strum Strum Strum Strum Strum Strum Strum Strum

1.4 HOW AND WHAT TO PRACTICE

How and What to Practice

Let's begin with our first official practice session. This book is designed to give you a clear practice plan to get you playing guitar quickly, as well as model for you what an ideal practice plan looks like. Each of the 10 lessons in this book is broken down into 6 days of practice, showing you exactly what to practice on each day.

Every practice session will include three elements: a warm-up, something new, and something to review. Make sure you don't skip any of these elements. The closer you can keep to the practice plan, the faster you will see results. All you need is 10 to 20 minutes per day, six days a week.

However, if it takes you longer to get through certain lessons, don't worry. Everyone learns differently. Some lessons may only take you a few minutes to get down, while others may take you a week or more. So don't think you have to rush or move on before you feel ready to.

Also, you don't have to play everything perfectly. Get as close to perfect as you can in 20 minutes or so and then move on. It takes time to learn the tools needed to make music, so relax and enjoy the process.

DAY 1 PRACTICE

Warm-Up:

For your first warm-up, simply tap your foot along with a metronome or a clock's second hand. Don't play anything yet; just feel the time and sync up with it. Do this for about a minute.

New:

Practice the following exercise changing from the Em chord to the G chord. Practice until there is little to no delay between the chord changes.

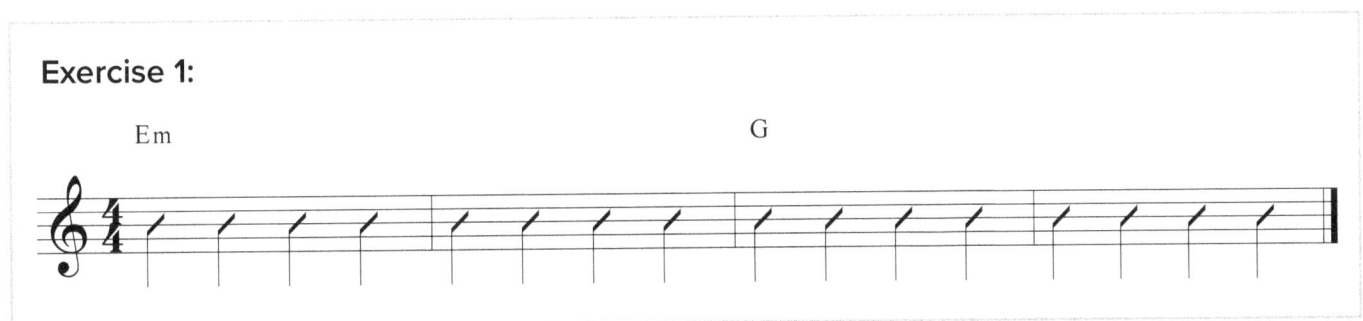

Exercise 1:

Review:

Play the three exercises under "Try It" on the previous page. Make sure to count out loud and play each chord as evenly and clearly as you can.

DAY 2 PRACTICE

Warm-Up:

For today's warm-up, simply tap your foot along with a metronome or a clock's second hand. Don't play anything yet, just feel the time and sync up with it. Do this for about a minute. (Same as Day 1.)

New:

Practice the following exercise.

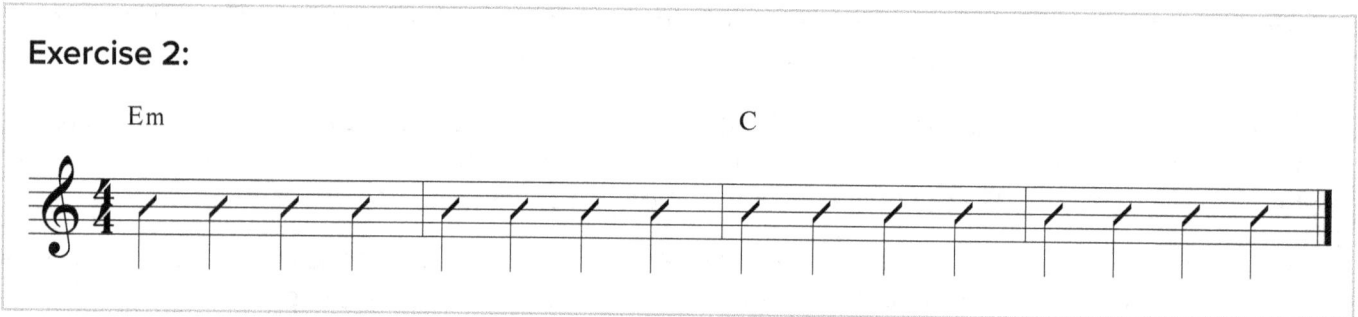

Review:

Play Exercise 1 and the three exercises under "Try It" found in section 1.34 (page 18).

DAY 3 PRACTICE

Warm-Up:

For today's warm-up, practice the "Try It" exercises found in section 1.34 (page 18).

New:

Practice the following exercise.

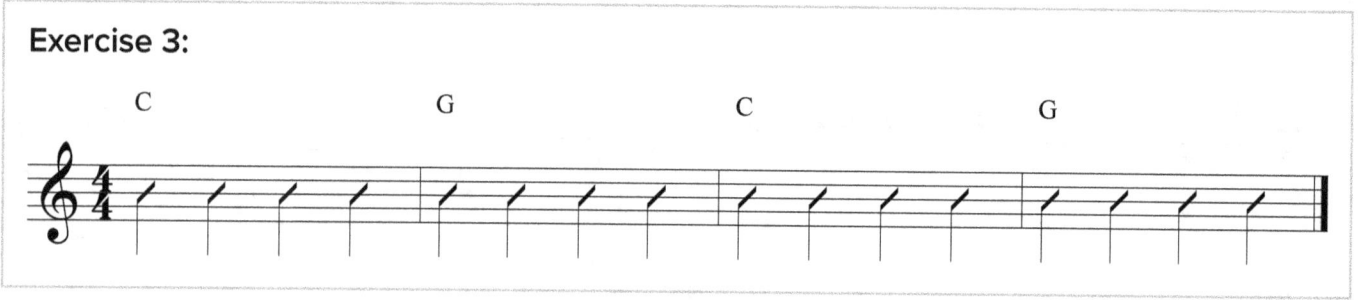

Review:

Go back and play Exercises 1 and 2.

DAY 4 PRACTICE

Warm-Up:

For today's warm-up, practice the "Try It" exercises found in section 1.34 (page 18).

New:

Practice the following exercise.

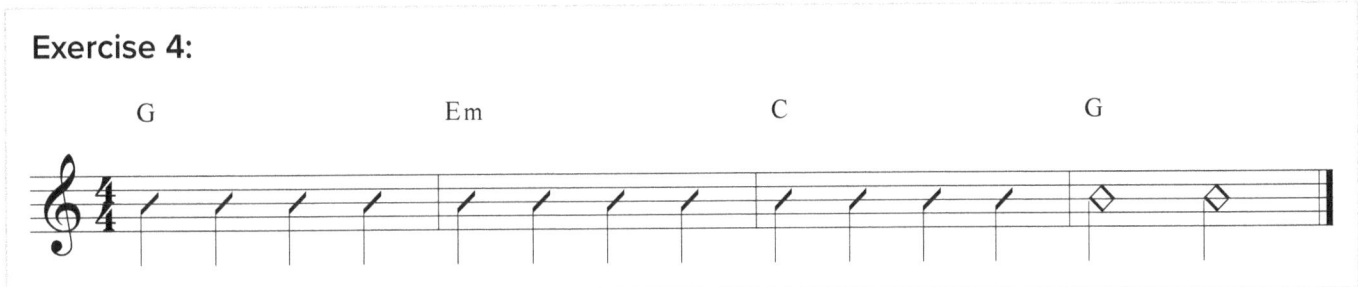

Review:

Play Exercises 1, 2, and 3.

DAY 5 PRACTICE

Warm-Up:

For today's warm-up, practice the "Try It" exercises found in section 1.34 (page 18).

New:

Practice the following exercise. This time you'll strum each chord only two times instead of four.

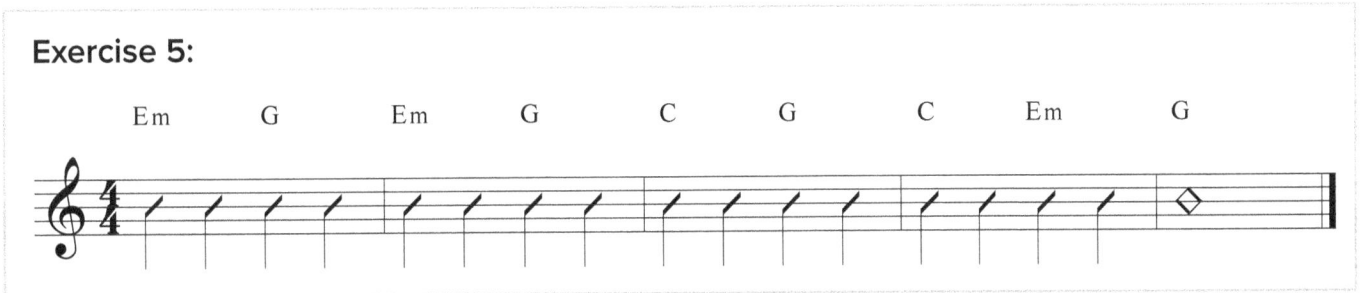

Review:

Play Exercises 1, 2, 3, and 4.

DAY 6 PRACTICE

Warm-Up:

For today's warm-up, practice Exercises 1 and 2 (pages 19 & 20).

New:

Practice the following exercise.

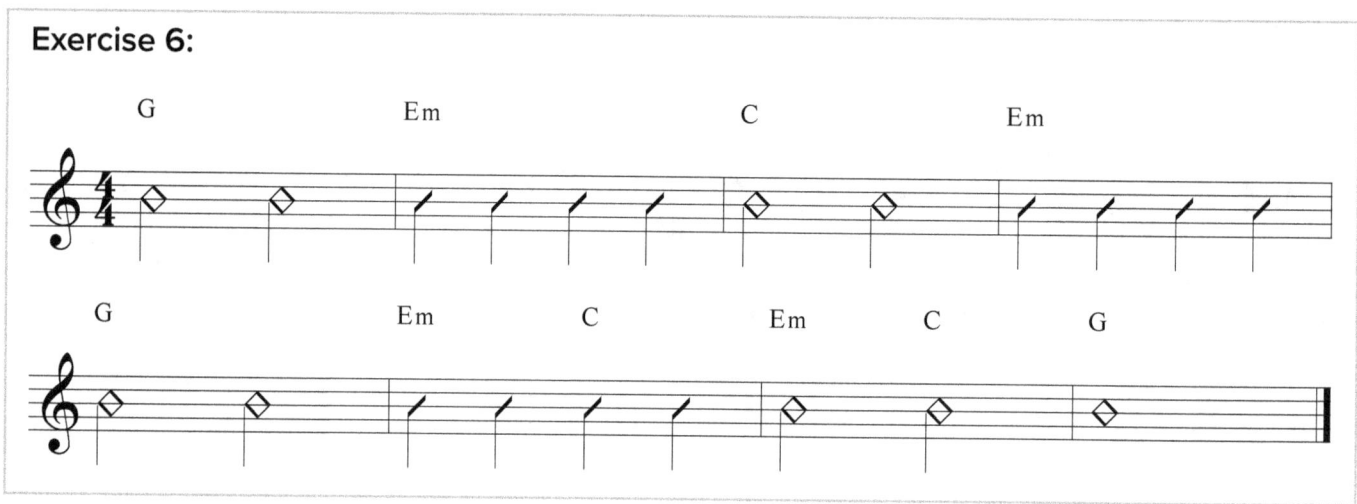

Review:

Play Exercises 3, 4, and 5.

LESSON 2

THE FULL Em, C, G, Am, & D CHORDS

In this lesson, we are going to expand your chords using more strings and more fingers for each chord. We will start by learning the full versions of Em, C, and G. Then you'll learn two new chords: Am and D.

Just as before, you'll first see what the chords look like. Then you'll try them out and learn them using the guided daily practice. Do note that many guitar students have trouble getting the full C and D chords at first. So keep your fingers on their tips, be patient, and know that with time and practice, you will get them.

DAY 1 PRACTICE: THE FULL Em CHORD

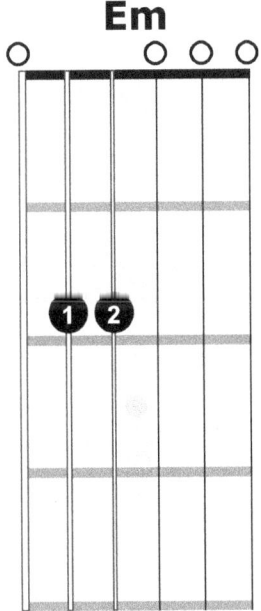

Try it: Practice strumming the following rhythm with the full Em chord shown above.

Warm-Up:

For today's warm-up, practice Exercise 5 from Lesson 1.

New:

Practice the following exercises. In Exercise 1, you'll be changing from the new Em chord to the G chord learned in Lesson 1. Exercise 2 is the same idea, but this time you are changing from the full Em to the C major chord learned in Lesson 1.

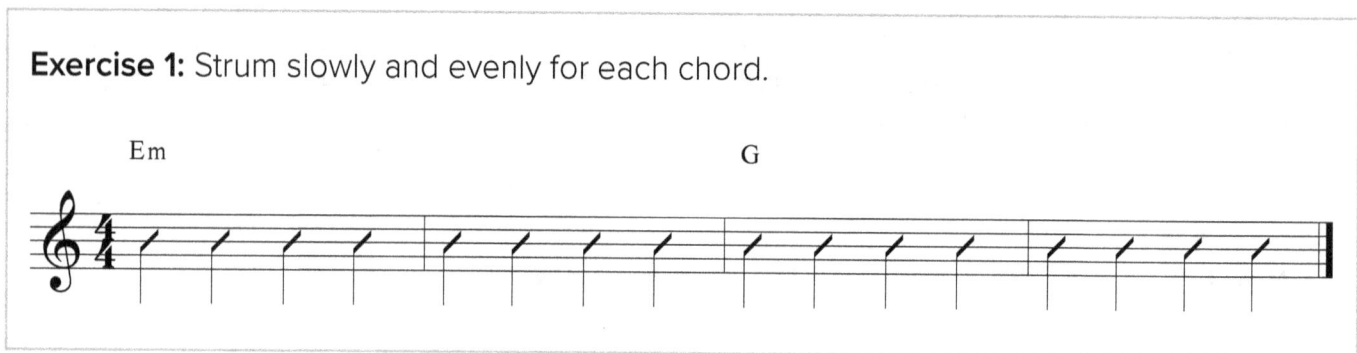

Exercise 1: Strum slowly and evenly for each chord.

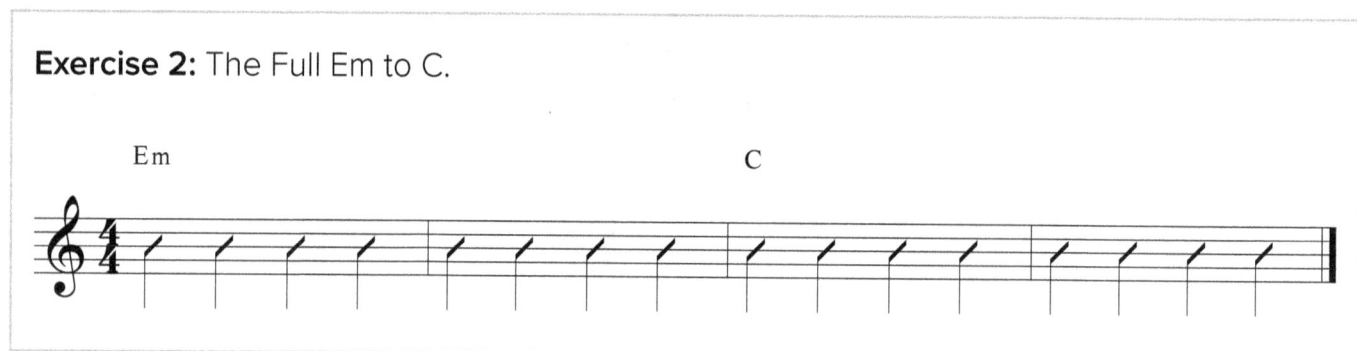

Exercise 2: The Full Em to C.

Review:

Play Exercise 6 from Lesson 1.

DAY 2 PRACTICE: THE FULL G CHORD

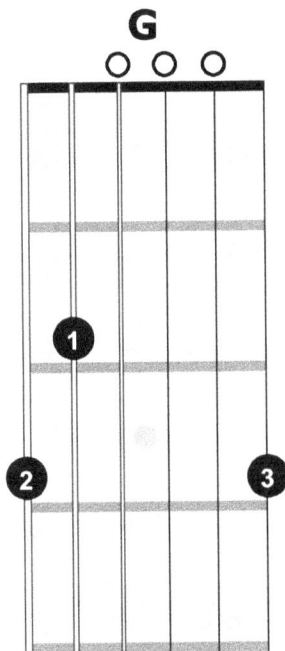

Try it: Practice strumming the full G chord with the following rhythms.

Warm-Up:

Review the full Em "Try It" section under Lesson 2 Day 1 Practice (page 23).

New:

Practice the Exercise 3 on the following page.

Exercise 3: G and Em have a common tone, so be sure to keep your index finger on the 5th string, 2nd fret for the entire exercise.

Review:

Play Exercises 1 and 2. Try using the new, full G chord in Exercise 1.

DAY 3 PRACTICE: THE FULL C CHORD

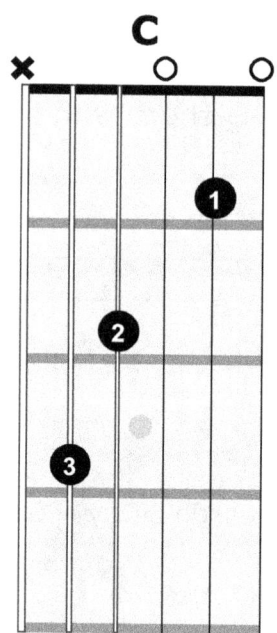

Try it: Practice strumming the following chord

Warm-Up:

For today's warm-up, practice the Em "Try It" (page 26) and the G Major "Try It" (page 25).

New:

Practice Exercise 4.

Exercise 4:

Between C and G there are no fingers held in place for both, so be sure to memorize each chord shape individually and work on transitioning as smoothly as you can. Keep in mind that it takes time to be able to do this easily.

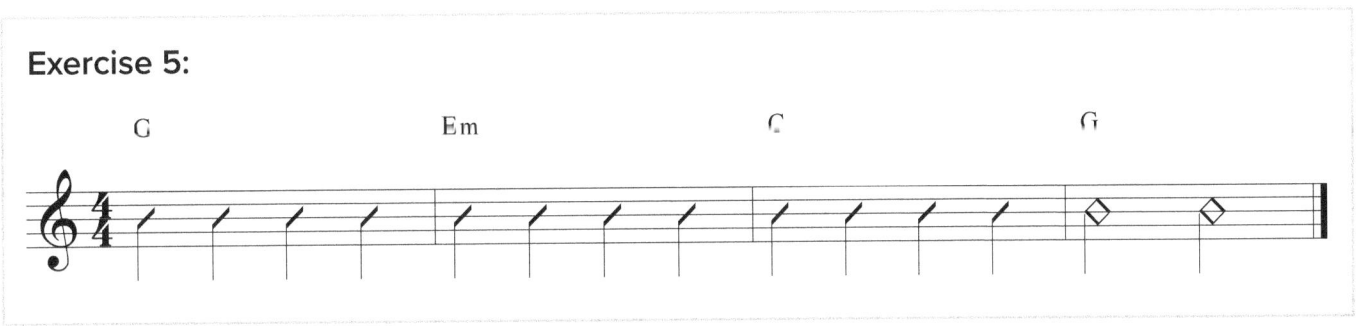

Review:

Use the following exercise to review the full Em, G, and C chords. Then go back and review Exercises 1-3. Be sure to now use the full G and C chords in Exercises 1 and 2.

Exercise 5:

DAY 4 PRACTICE: THE Am CHORD

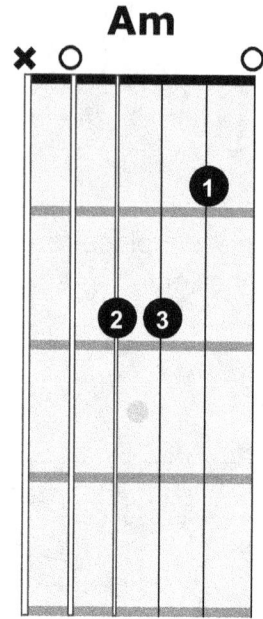

Try it: Practice strumming the Am chord below.

Warm-Up:

For today's warm-up, practice the "Try It" sections for the Em, C, G, and Am chords.

New:

Learn the chord Am using the following exercises.

Exercise 6:

Between the Am and C there are two common tones. To move from Am to C, simply remove the 3rd finger from the 3rd string (2nd fret) and place it on the 5th string (3rd fret).

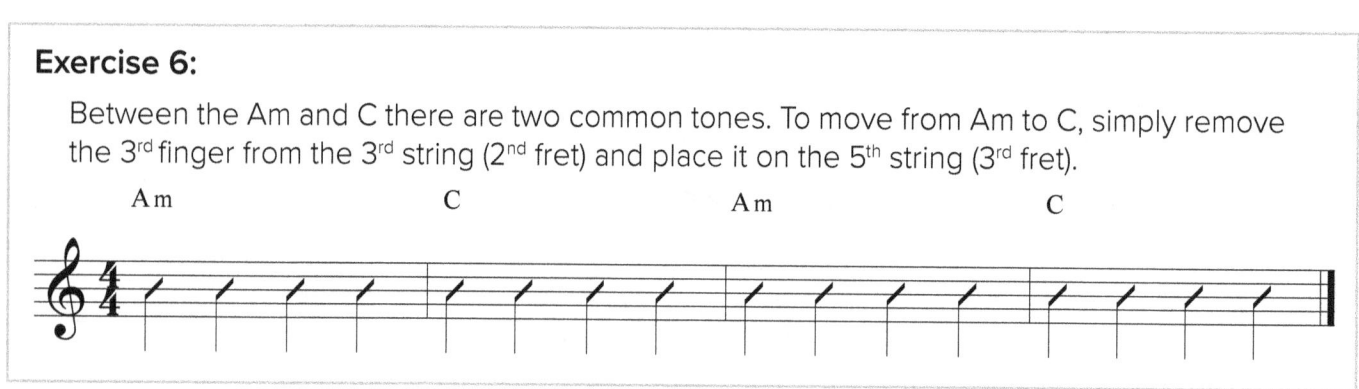

Exercise 7:

When changing from an Am to an Em, remove the first finger and then place your other two fingers onto strings 5 and 4, both on the second fret. (Note that this fingering differs from the chord chart, but works well in this application.)

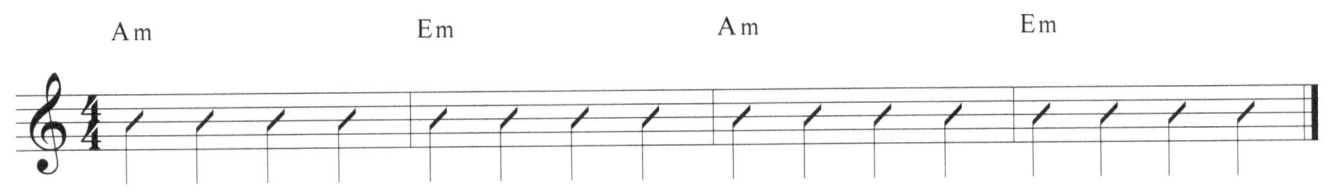

Review:

Play Exercises 1, 2, 3, 4, and 5.

DAY 5 PRACTICE: THE D CHORD

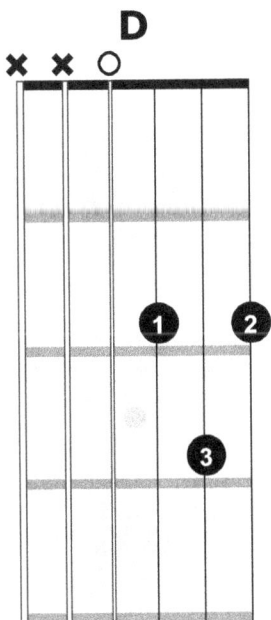

Try it: Practice strumming the D chord below.

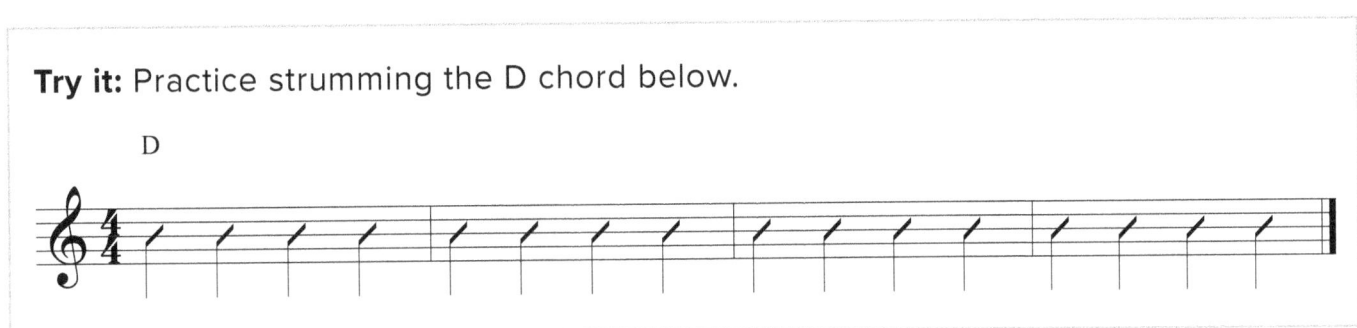

Warm-Up:

For today's warm-up, play Exercises 1 and 2.

New:

Practice Exercises 8 & 9.

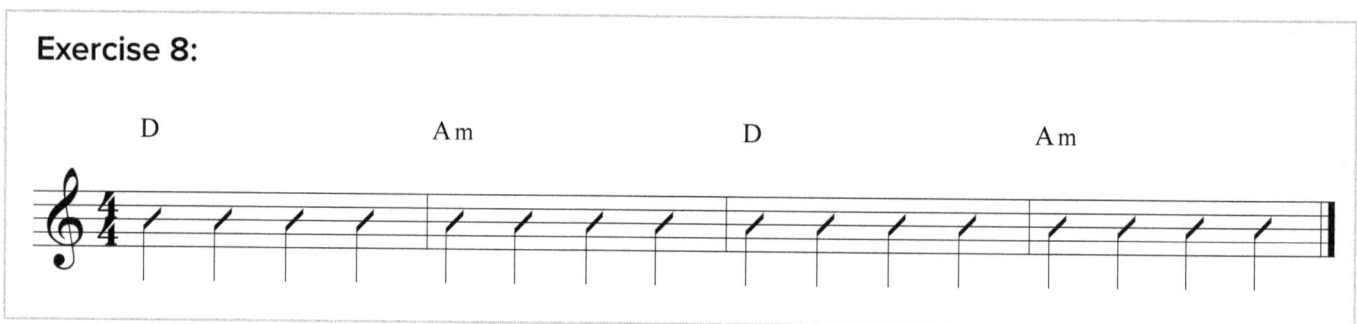

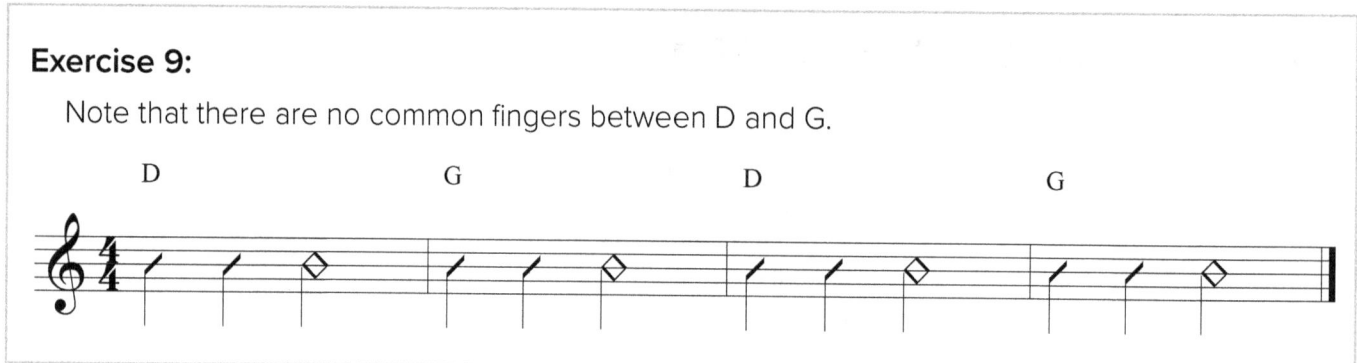

Review:

Play Exercises 3, 4, 5, 6, and 7.

DAY 6 PRACTICE: A COMMON CHORD PROGRESSION

Warm-Up:

For today's warm-up, play Exercises 1, 2, 3, and 4.

New:

Practice the following exercises. Exercises 10 and 11 are common chord progressions, meaning that they are standard sets of chords used in a countless number of songs. They may even sound familiar to you.

Exercise 10:

Practice this common chord progression.

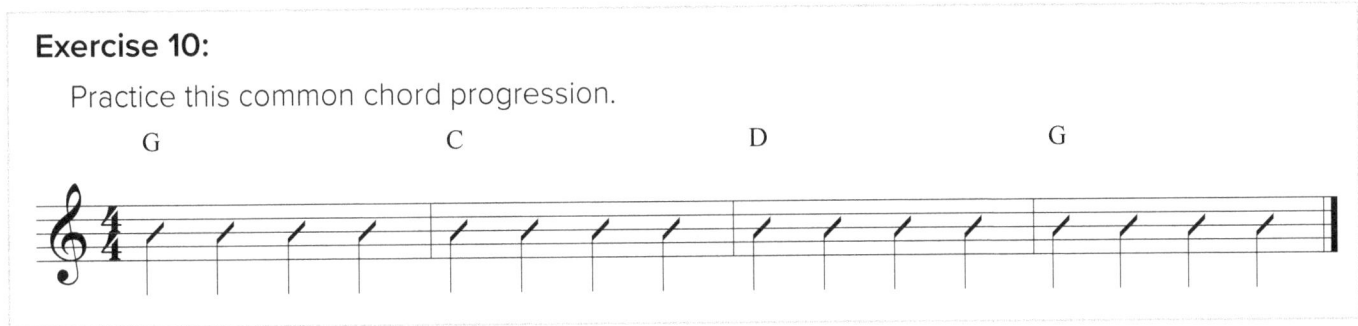

Exercise 11:

Use the following exercise to review all the chords you've learned so far.

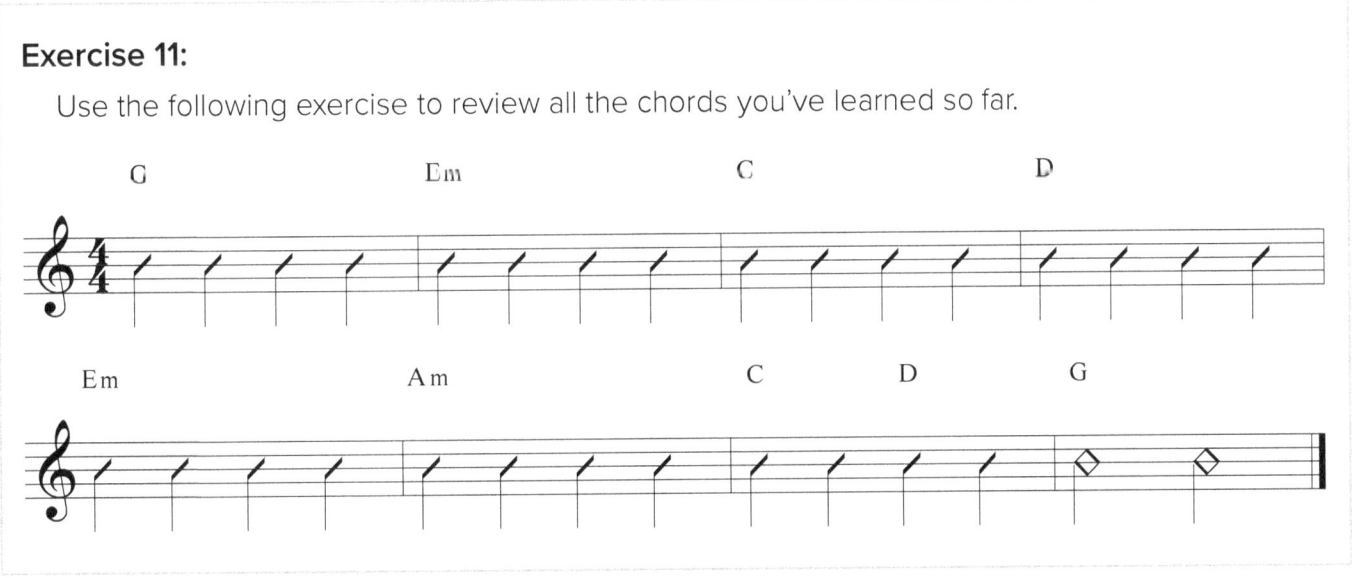

Review:

Play Exercises 5, 6, 7, 8, and 9.

LESSON 3

THE A, D7, E, AND B7 CHORDS & EIGHTH NOTE STRUMMING

In this lesson, we will continue to expand your knowledge of the most commonly played guitar chords, covering the chords A, D7, E, and B7. Do note that the B7 chord is the rare beginner chord that uses four fingers. Also in this lesson, you'll learn how to strum eighth notes, giving you more options for strumming.

You may wonder why the chords seem to be presented in a random order. They are not. The chords that have been selected for this book are presented in a way that will allow you to build finger strength as you learn them and use them in a musical context. So chords that appear to be missing, like a C minor for example, are not included because they are much harder for beginner guitarists to play. Do note that a chord chart featuring all the chords learned in this book plus a few more can be found at the end of the book.

DAY 1 PRACTICE: THE A CHORD

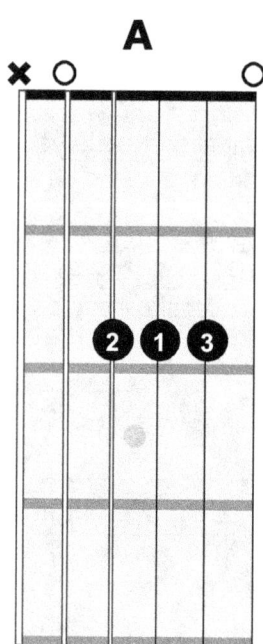

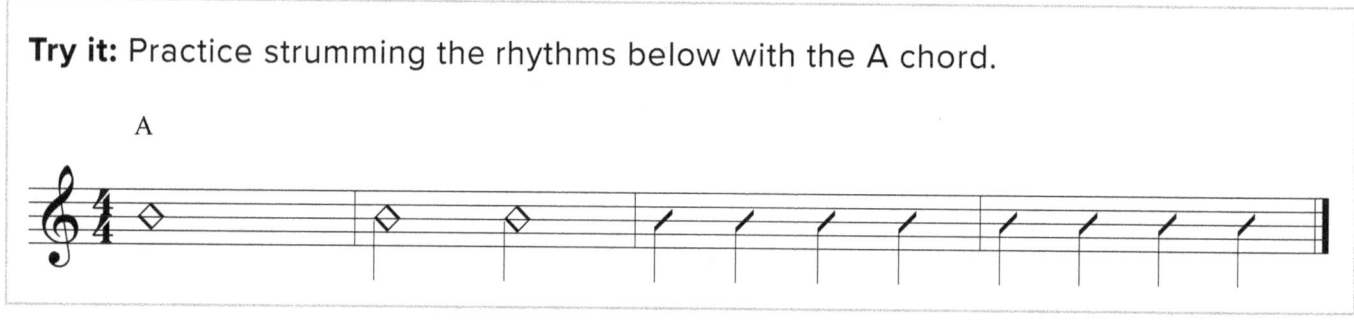

Try it: Practice strumming the rhythms below with the A chord.

Warm-Up:

Play Lesson 2, Exercise 11.

New:

Practice the following exercises. In Exercise 1, you'll be using the new A major chord along with the D chord from Lesson 2. In Exercise 2, you'll be playing A major followed by A minor to help you learn the difference between them.

Exercise 1:

When moving from A to D, keep the index finger in place using it a pivot note.

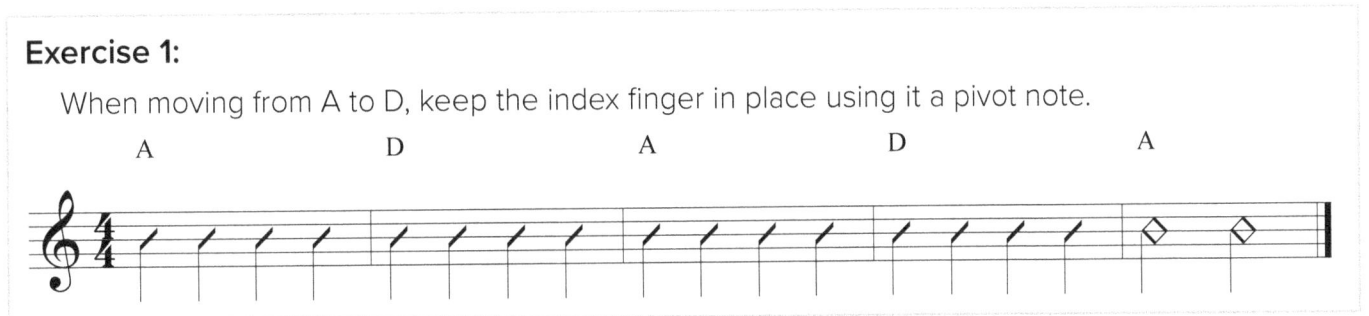

Exercise 2:

When moving from A to Am, keep the middle finger in place using it a pivot note. You will have to make a tiny adjustment, but the finger doesn't need to be removed from the fret to do so.

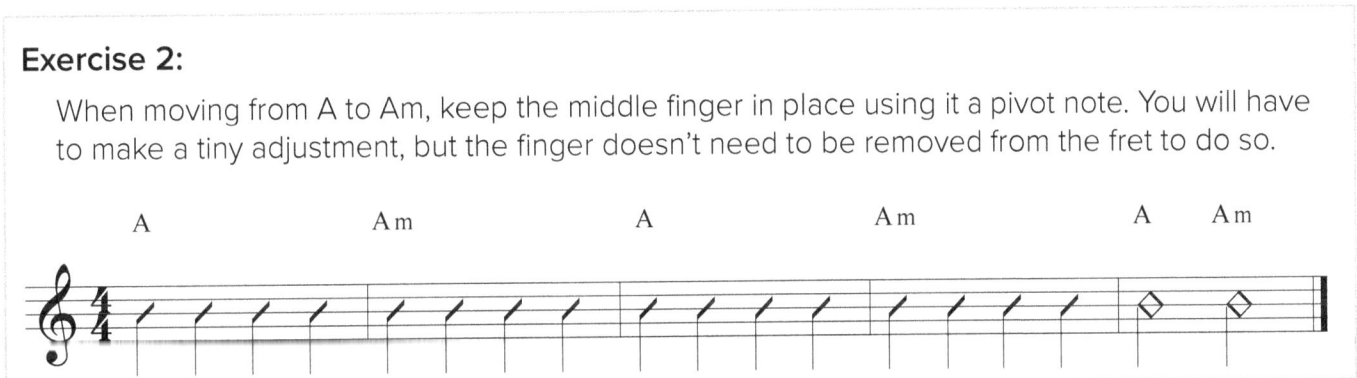

Review:

Play Exercises 6, 7, 8, and 9 from Lesson 2.

DAY 2 PRACTICE: THE D7 CHORD

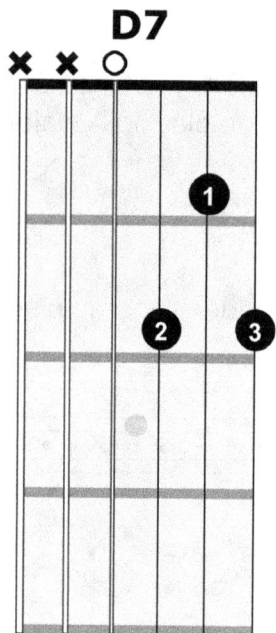

Try it: Practice strumming the rhythms below with the D7 chord.

Warm-Up:

Play Lesson 2, Exercise 11 and the A Major "Try It."

New:

Practice the following exercises.

Exercise 3:

Between D7 and A there are no common fingers. However, they are near each other, so look for the most efficient way to move from one to the other.

Exercise 4:
Now practice the D7 with the G and Am chords learned in Lesson 2. Notice that you don't have to move your index finger when switching from D7 to Am.

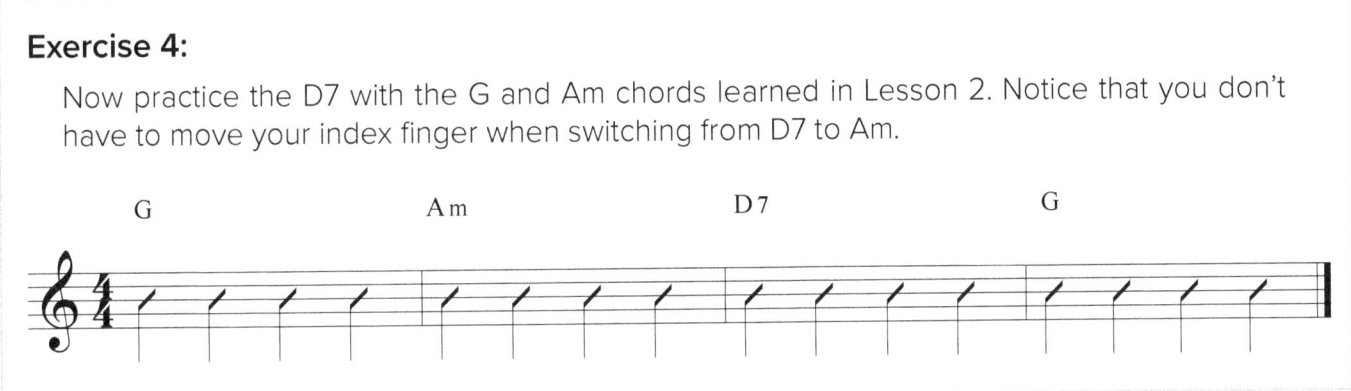

Review:

Play Exercises 1 and 2. Then play Exercises 10 and 11 from Lesson 2.

DAY 3 PRACTICE: THE E CHORD

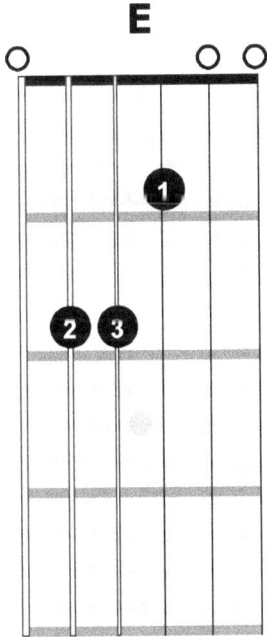

Try it: Practice strumming the rhythms below with the E chord.

Warm-Up:

Play the A major "Try It" and the D7 "Try It."

New:

Practice the following exercises.

Exercise 5:

Practice moving between the E and A chords. Note this is A major and not Am.

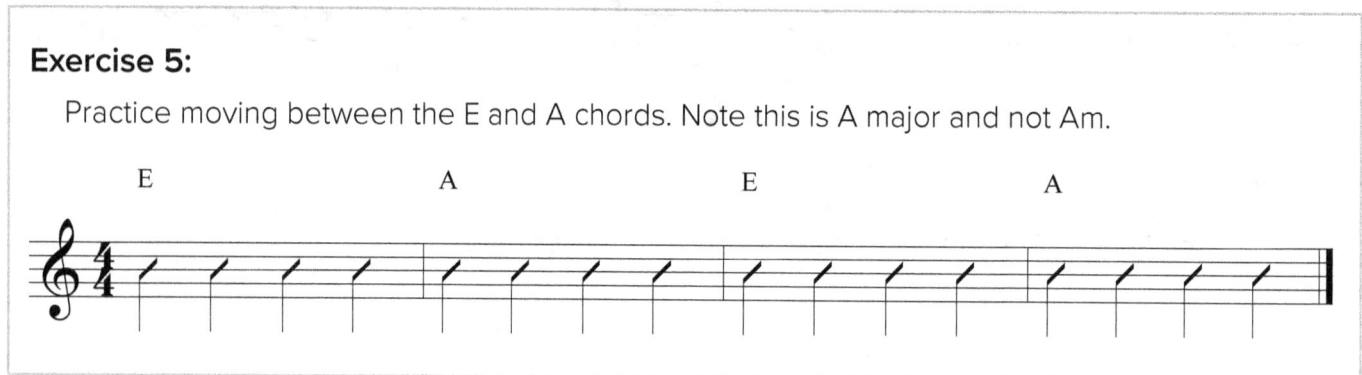

Exercise 6:

Practice moving between the E major and Em chords.

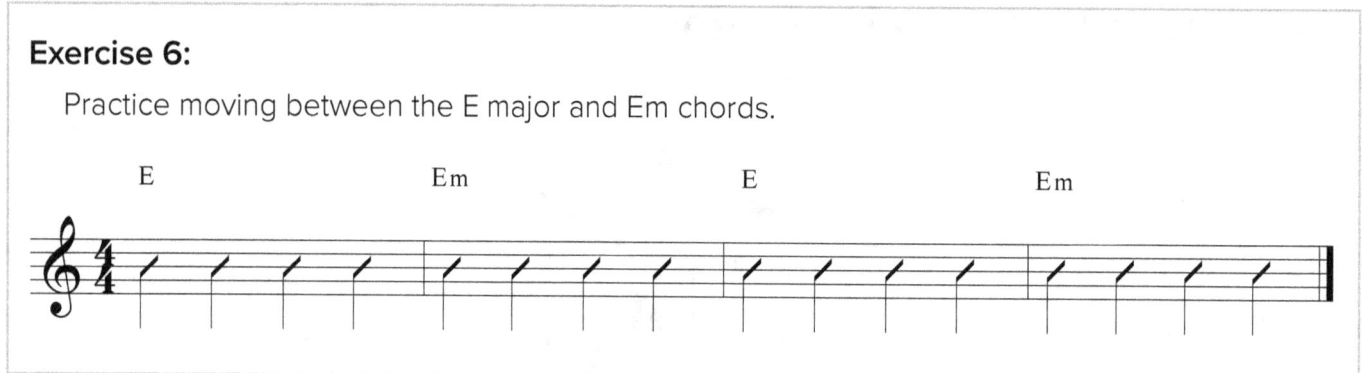

Review:

Play Exercises 1, 2, 3 and 4.

DAY 4 PRACTICE: THE B7 CHORD

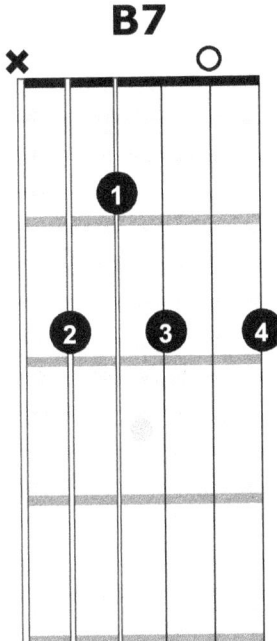

Try it: Practice strumming the rhythms below with the B7 chord.

Warm-Up:

Play Exercises 1 and 2.

New:

Practice the following, Exercises 7 & 8.

Exercise 7:

Practice moving between the B7 and E major chords.

Exercise 8:

Practice the B7, E, and A chords.

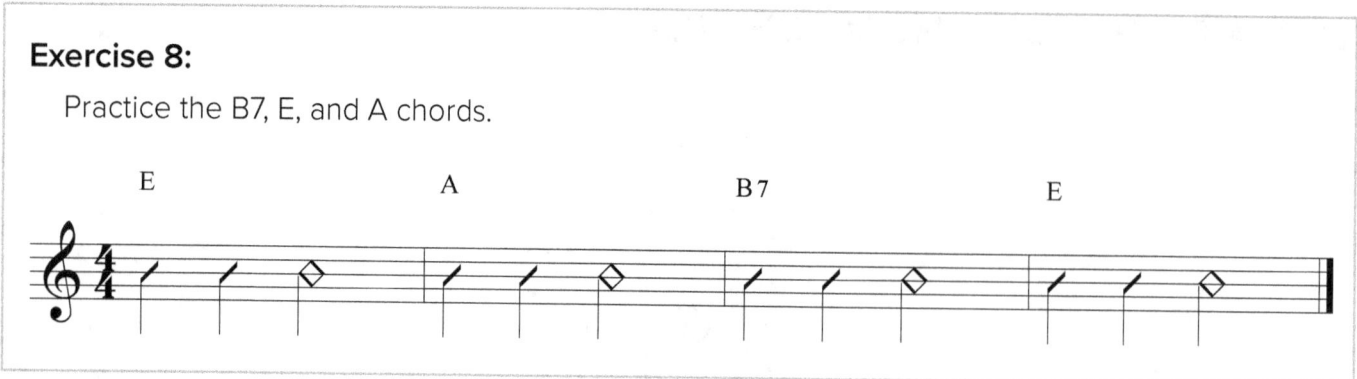

Review:

Use the following exercise to review all the chords learned so far.

Exercise 9:

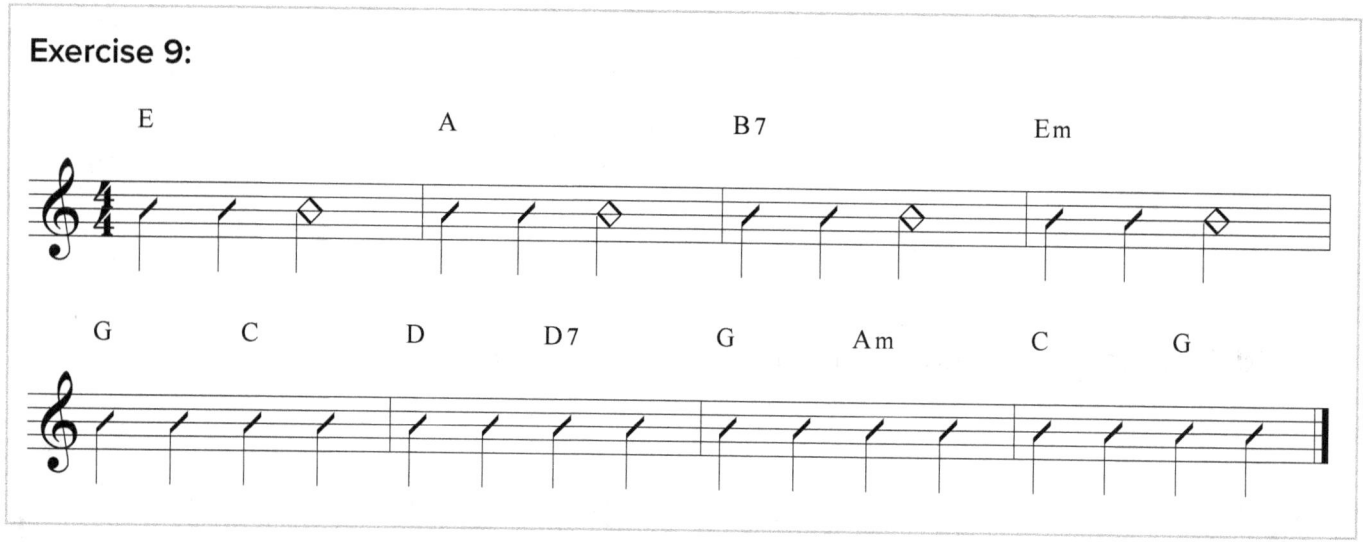

DAY 5 PRACTICE: EIGHTH NOTE STRUMMING

For Day 5 Practice we are going to learn how to strum eighth notes. So first, you'll want to understand what an eighth note is and how to play it. Let's begin with a review of quarter notes. Follow the diagram below to guide you as you strum.

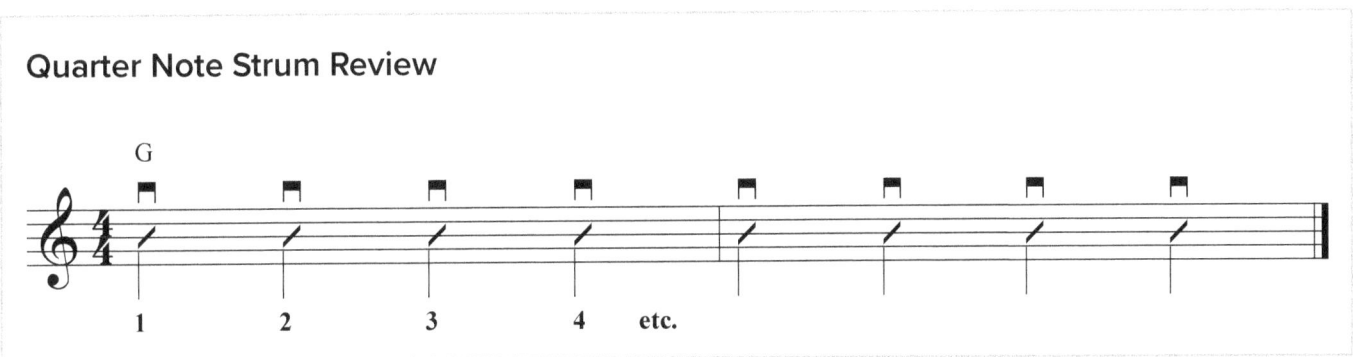

In the above example, each quarter note strum represents one full beat. We can divide each one of those beats in half. When this is done, the resulting notes are called eighth notes (see below). The eighth notes are always connected with a line at the top. A single eighth note will look like a quarter note with a flag on it.

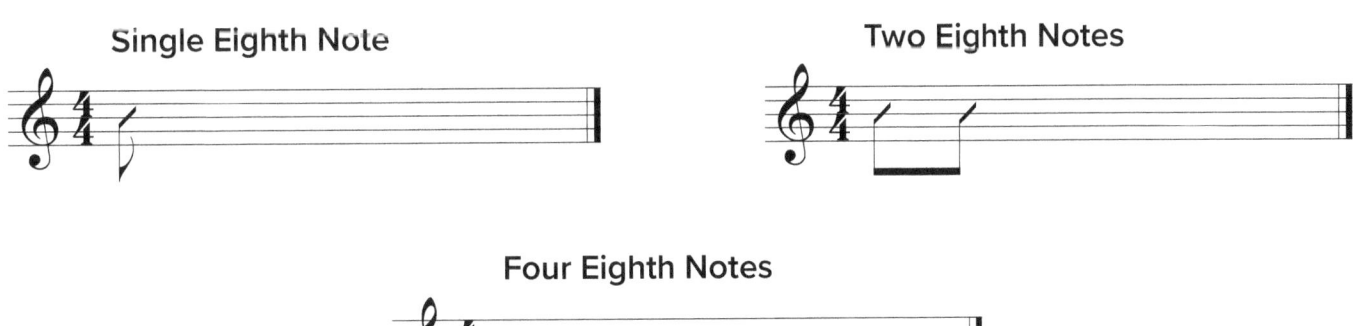

When strumming eighth notes, you strum the first half of the beat downward and the second half of each beat upward. So as you strum, think: "down-up, down-up, down-up, down-up." Therefore, you are playing on the beat for the down strum, and off the beat for the up strum.

Try it: Practice strumming eighth notes

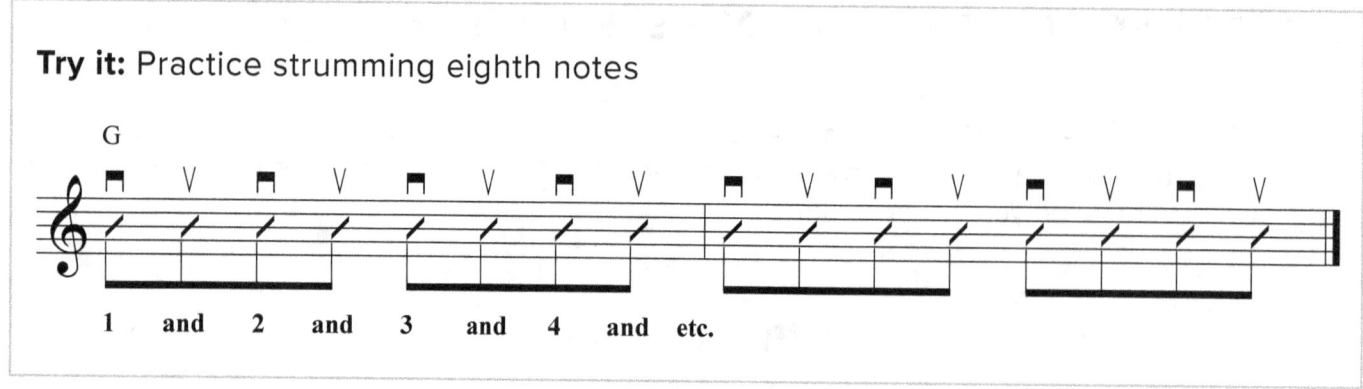

Warm-Up:

Play Exercises 1, 2, 3, and 4.

New:

Practice the following eighth note exercise.

Exercise 10:

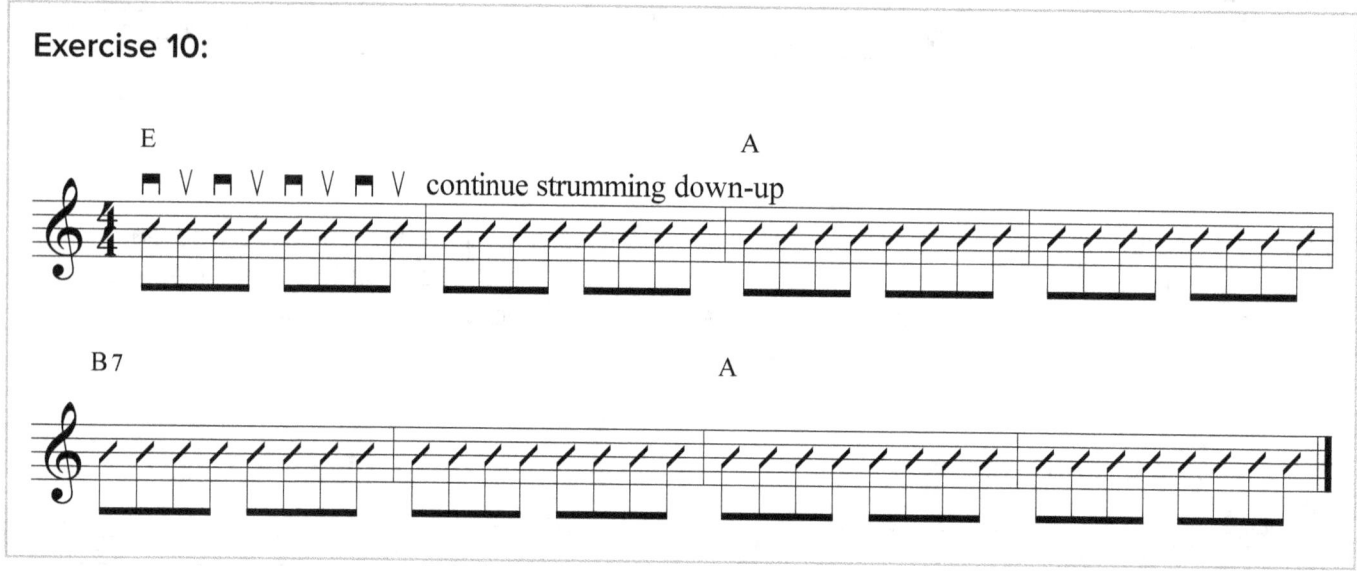

Review:

Play Exercise 9.

DAY 6 PRACTICE: COMBINING RHYTHMS

For today's practice, work on strumming quarter notes and eighth notes. Remember the eighth notes are twice the speed of quarter notes, so it takes to two eighth notes to take up the same space as a quarter note, so be careful not to rush the quarter notes.

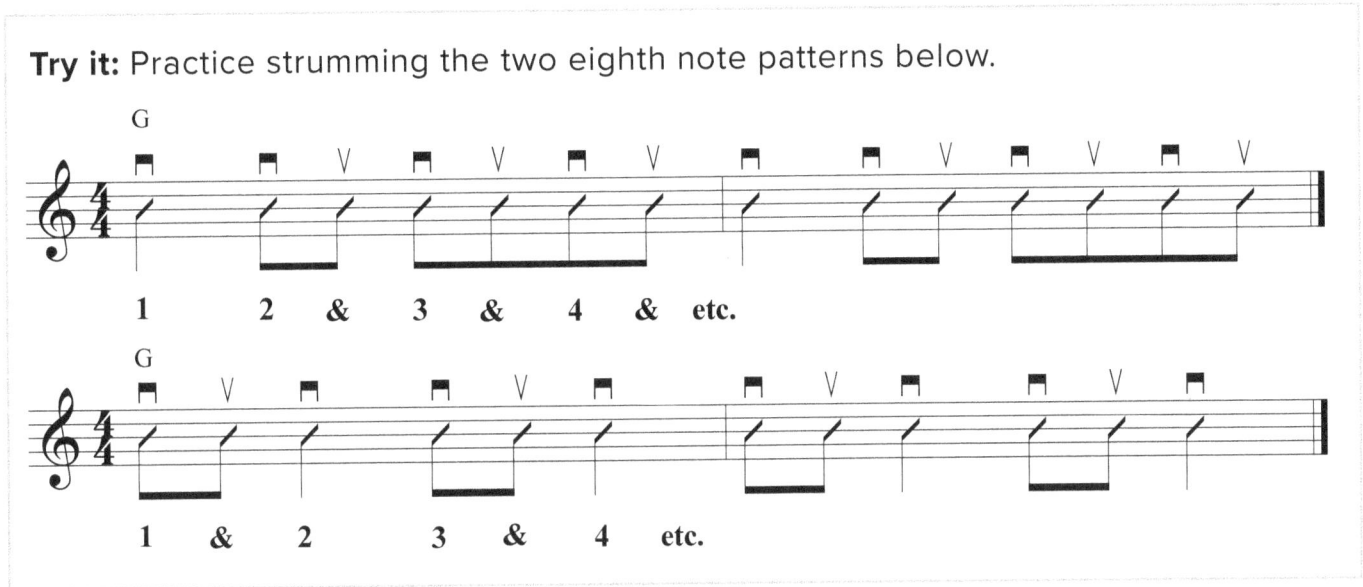

Try it: Practice strumming the two eighth note patterns below.

Warm-Up:

Play Exercises 7, 8, and 9.

New:

Practice the following eighth note exercises (Exercises 11 & 12).

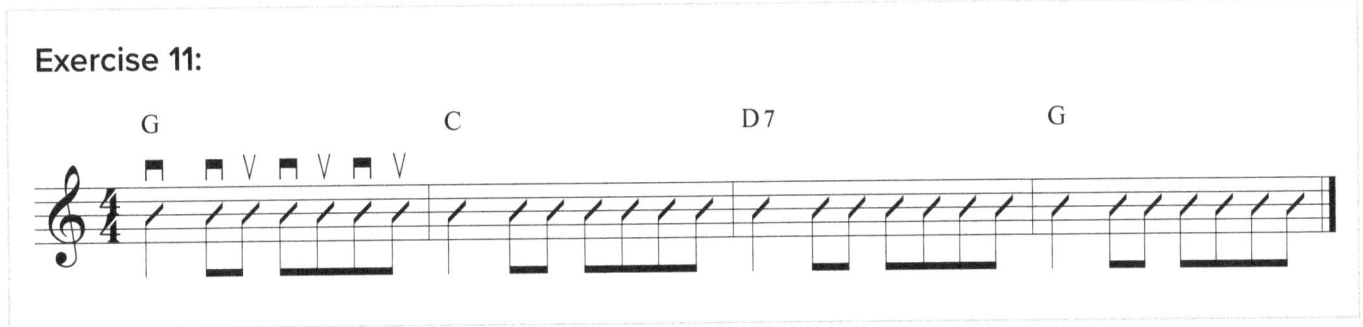

Exercise 11:

Exercise 12:

Practice the following strum pattern with all the chords from this lesson.

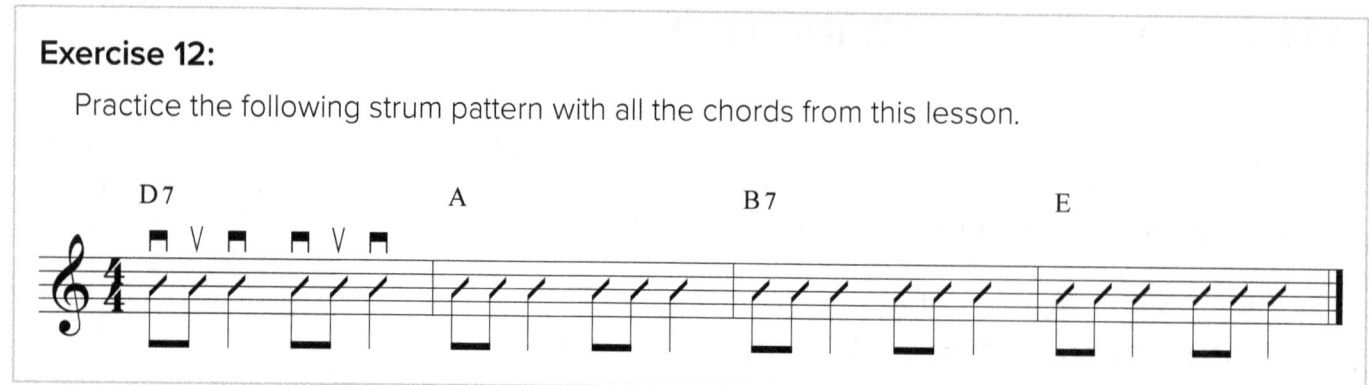

Review:

Play Exercises 1-10.

LESSON 4

THE FULL F CHORD & CHORD PROGRESSIONS

In this lesson we'll be covering two different topics. First, we'll take on one more chord, the "F" major chord. Second, we'll talk about chord progressions, including what they are and how to use them.

DAY 1 PRACTICE: THE F MAJOR CHORD

Since learning to play the F major chord can be a challenge for most players, it's a good idea to start it off with a slightly easier three-string version. It is still a complete F chord, but it doesn't sound as full. Notice that the first string isn't played. To do this, simply lean your first finger onto the first string. That way you can still strum the string, but you'll be muting its sound.

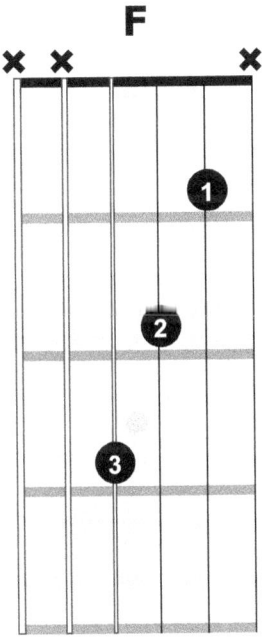

Try it: Practice strumming the following.

Warm-Up:

Play the "Try It" section from Lesson 3, Day 6.

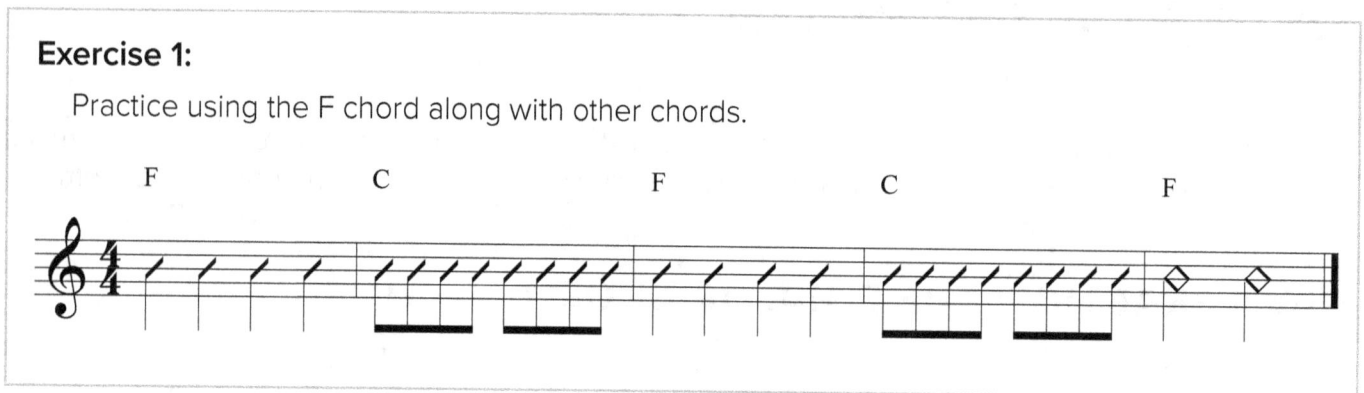

Review:

Play Exercises 11 and 12 from Lesson 3.

DAY 2 PRACTICE: THE FULL F MAJOR CHORD

The full F major chord is technically a **barre chord**. A barre chord is any chord that uses one finger to hold down more than one string.

In the case of F major, you will be using your index finger to hold down both strings 1 and 2 at the first fret. Once this finger is in place, put your other two fingers down. Keep your wrist dropped and your fingers spread apart so they are not touching each other. You don't want to grip the neck.

Again, it takes time to build up the finger strength needed to make this chord work, so as you practice you may want to switch between the full F chord and the easier three-note F chord in order to comfortably play through a series of chords.

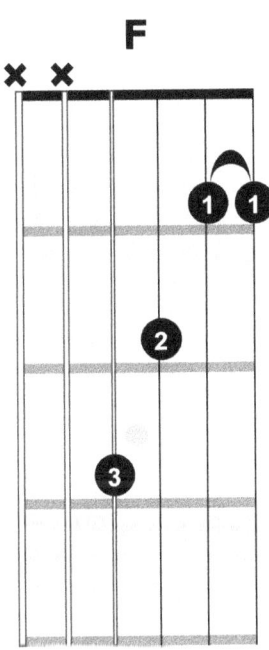

Try it: Practice strumming the F Major Chord.

Warm-Up:

Play the "Try It" section from Lesson 3, Day 6.

New:

Practice the following exercises.

Exercise 2:

Practice using the full F chord along with the C chord.

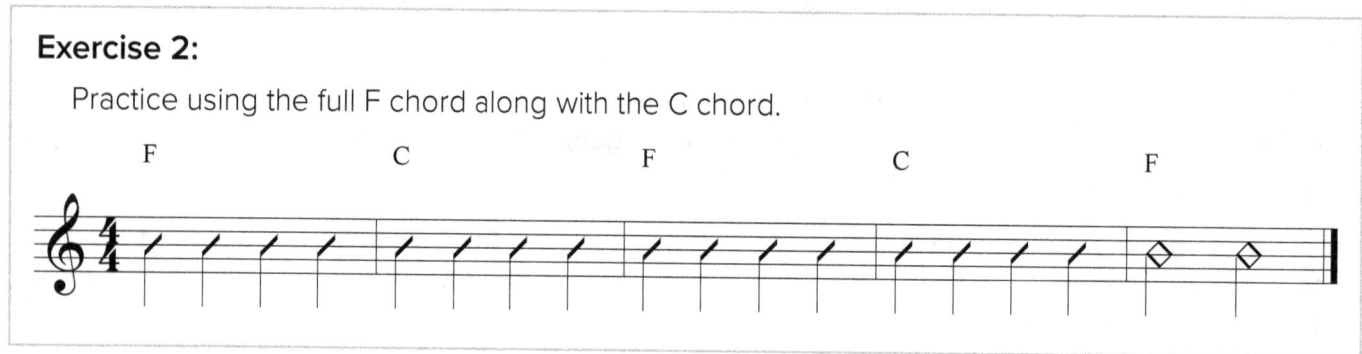

Exercise 3:

Practice using the full F chord with G and C.

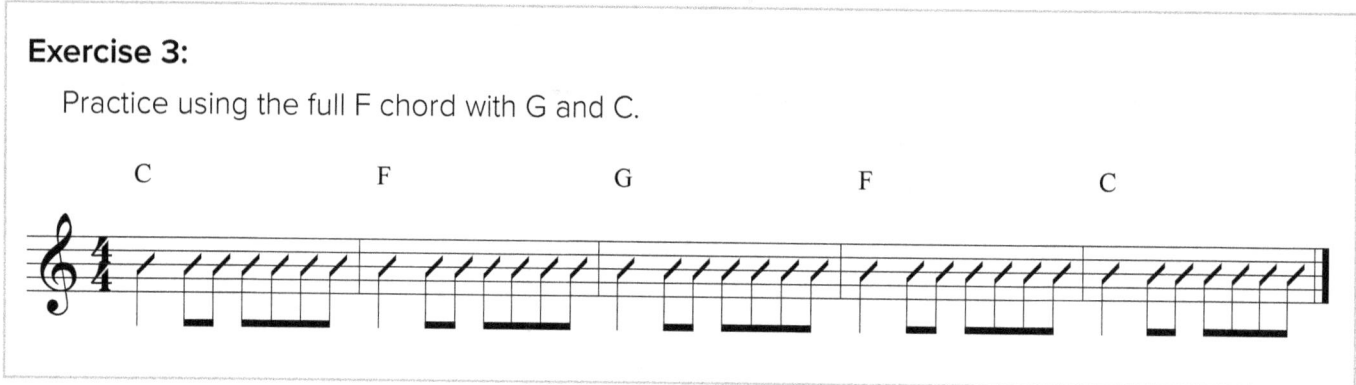

Review:

Play Exercise 1, then go back and play Exercises 11 and 12 from Lesson 3.

DAY 3 PRACTICE: CHORD PROGRESSIONS

So far in this book you've learned 10 of the most commonly used chords on the guitar. (You can find some of the other most common chords on the chord list in the back of the book.)

In most music, chords typically follow certain rules and patterns that sound good. Therefore, when starting to play guitar, it is helpful to get used to these familiar patterns of chords. These series of chords are called **chord progressions**, meaning that the chords have a starting, middle, and end point that can be repeated continuously to create a song. There are of course many, many exceptions and different approaches to playing chords, but as an acoustic guitar player, learning these chord progressions can be incredibly useful.

Warm-Up:

Play the Day 2 Practice "Try It."

New:

Practice the following chord progression exercises.

Exercise 4:

The Most Common Chord Progression on guitar. Version 1.

Exercise 5:

The Most Common Chord Progression on guitar. Version 2.

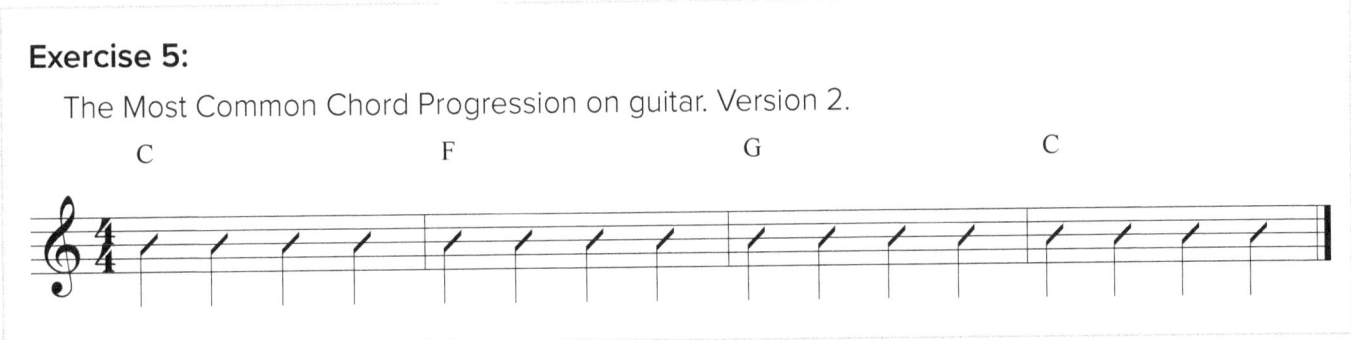

Notice how Exercises 4 & 5 sound about the same, but use a different set of chords. The reason for this gets technical pretty quickly. Just know that these chords always sound good together and are found like this in a countless number of songs.

Review:

Play Exercises 1, 2, and 3, using the full F chord whenever possible.

DAY 4 PRACTICE: THE TURNAROUND & THE REPEAT SIGN

Today's chord progression is called "the **turnaround**." It uses a group of related chords in such a way to make it sound like it should start over or loop.

At the end of today's new exercise (Exercise 6) you'll notice two dots next to the double bar line. These two dots are called the **repeat sign.** This simply means you'll repeat the entire exercise.

Warm-Up:

Play Exercise 12 from Lesson 3 and the "Try It" from Day 2.

New:

Practice the following chord progression exercises.

Exercise 6:
The Turnaround starting on G with the repeat sign.

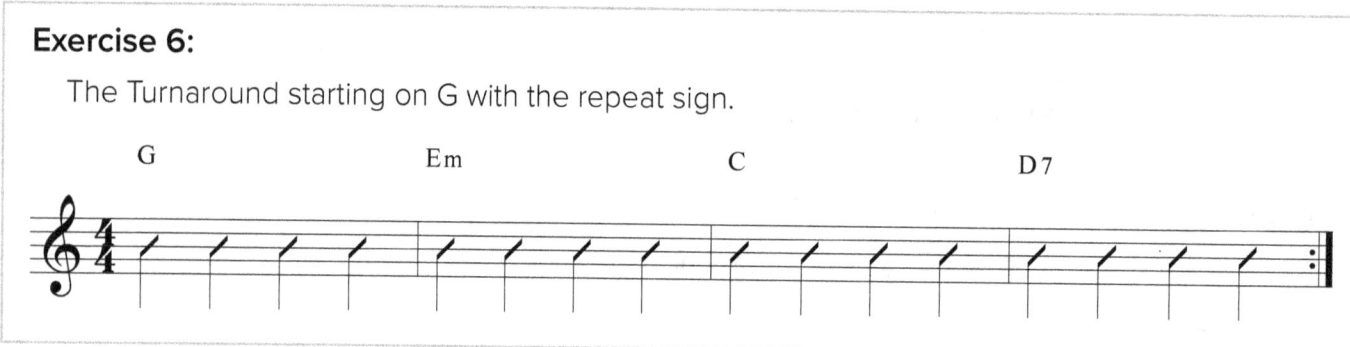

Exercise 7:
The Turnaround starting on C with the repeat sign.

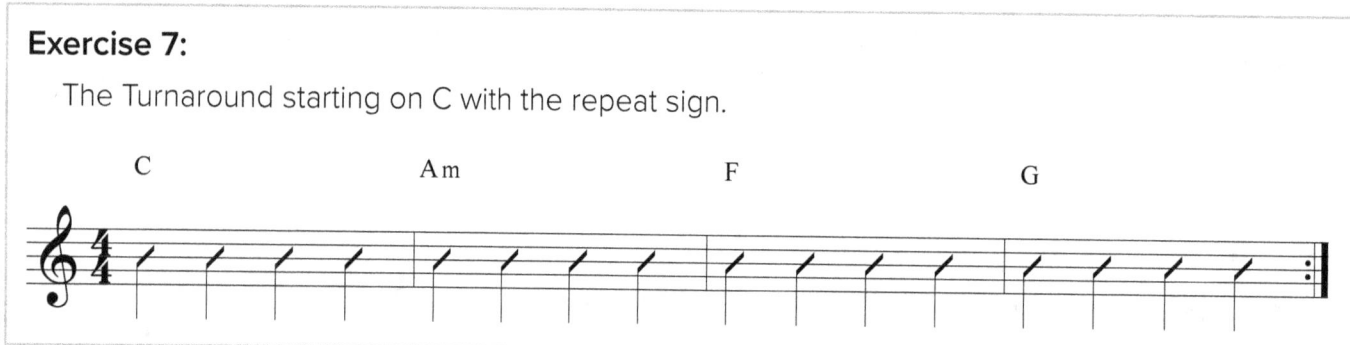

Exercise 8:
The same turnaround from Exercise 7 but with eighth notes.

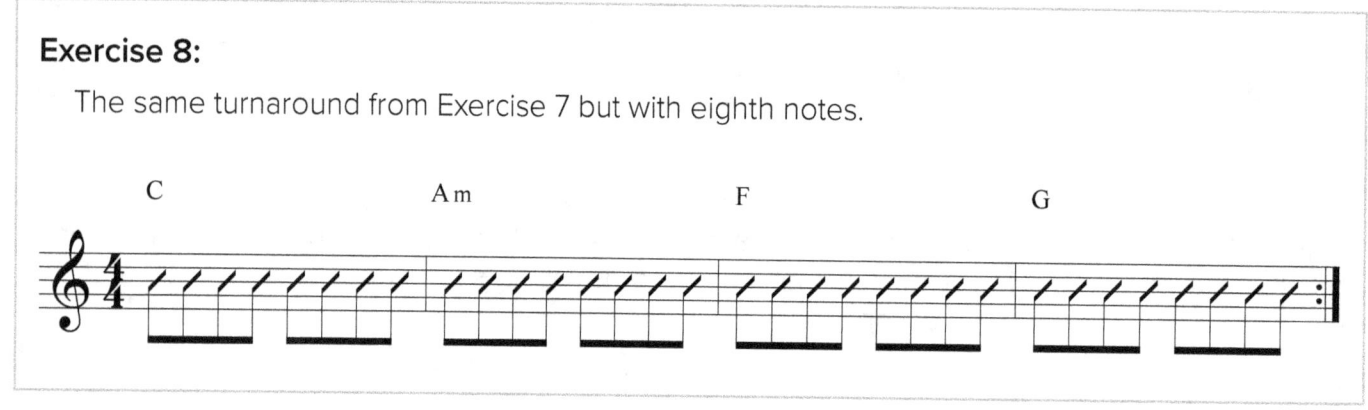

Review:

Play Exercises 2 and 3, using the full F chord. Also review Exercises 4 and 5.

DAY 5 PRACTICE: CHORD PROGRESSION 3 & TURNAROUND 2

Warm-Up:

Play Exercises 1, 2, and 3.

New:

Practice the following chord progression exercises.

Exercise 9: Turnaround 2 Starting on G.

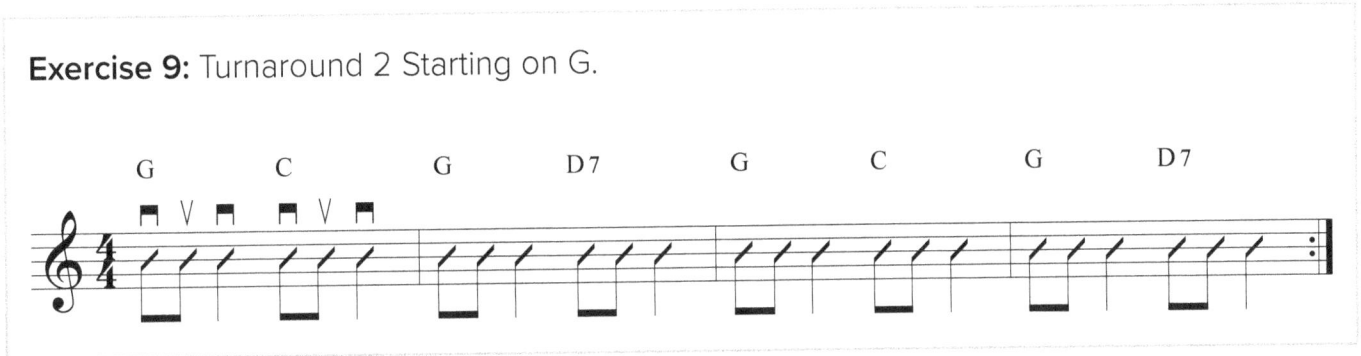

Exercise 10:

Turnaround 2 Starting on C. Notice the new strum pattern present here. Count it like this: "One, Two-And, Three, Four-And" or "Down, Down-Up, Down, Down-Up."

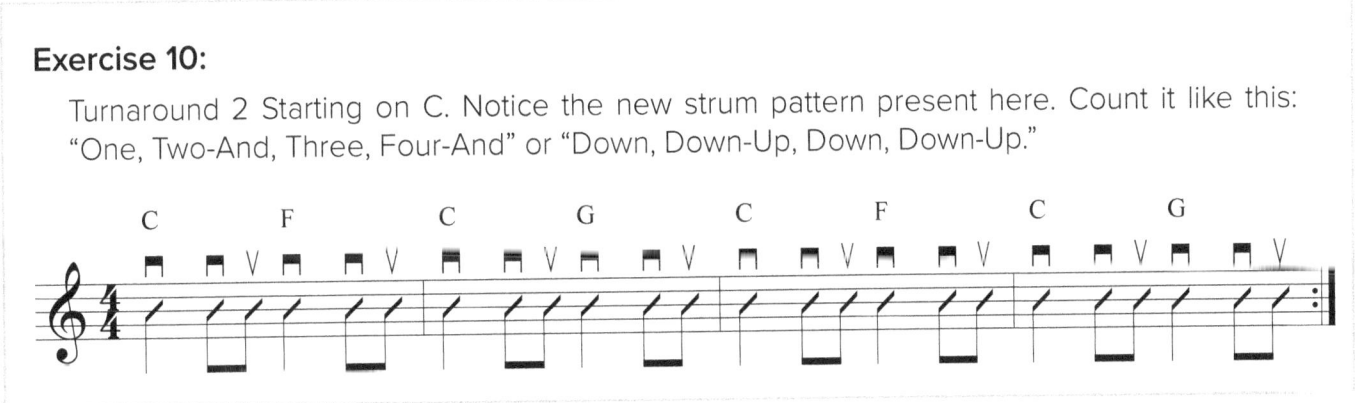

Review:

Play Exercises 4, 5, 6, 7, and 8.

DAY 6 PRACTICE: CHORD PROGRESSION 4, THE 12-BAR BLUES

Today's chord progression is called "The 12-Bar Blues." It takes the chord progression from Day 3 and applies it to a widely used song form called "The 12-Bar Blues." As the name so clearly states, it is a 12 measure chord progression that originated in blues music, but has since been adopted by just about every kind of music. Because of this, it may sound like you've heard it before.

Warm-Up:

Play Exercises 2, 3, 4, and 5.

New:

Practice the following chord progression exercises, Exercises 11 & 12.

Exercise 11:

The Basic 12-Bar Blues Starting on G.

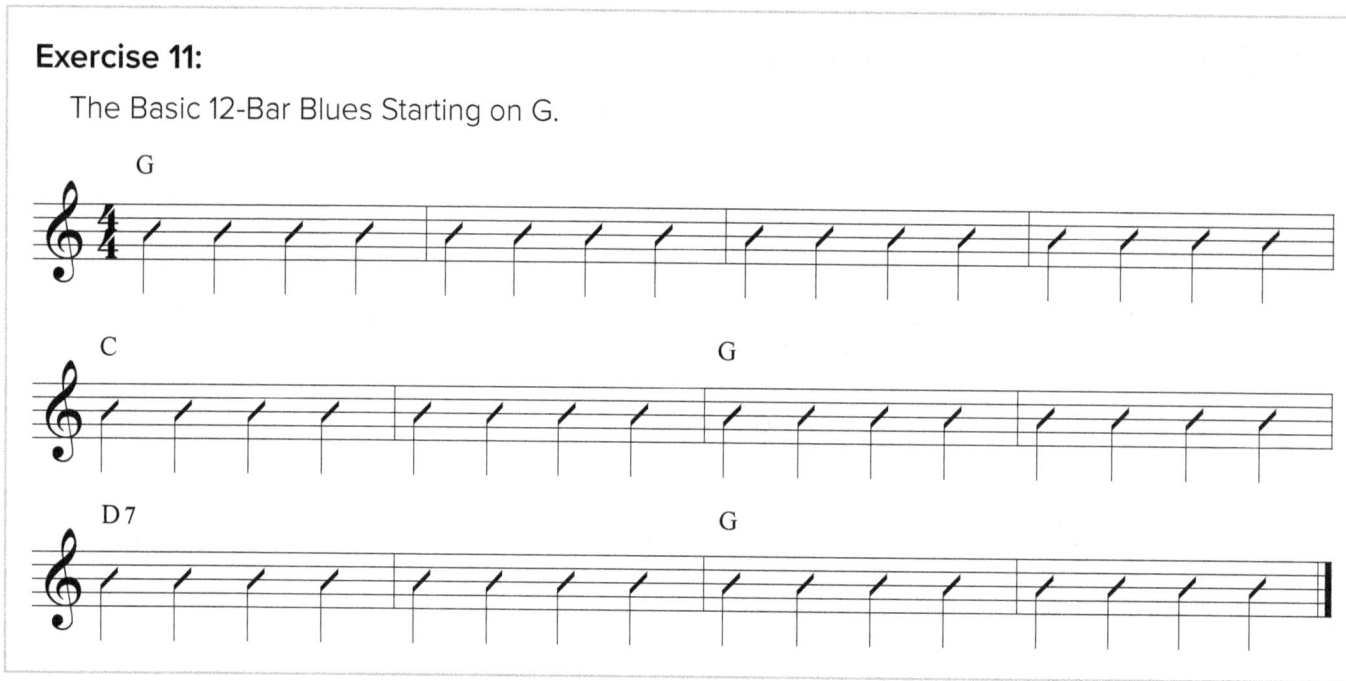

Exercise 12:

The 12-Bar Blues Starting on C. Note the repeat sign and the turnaround in the last two measures.

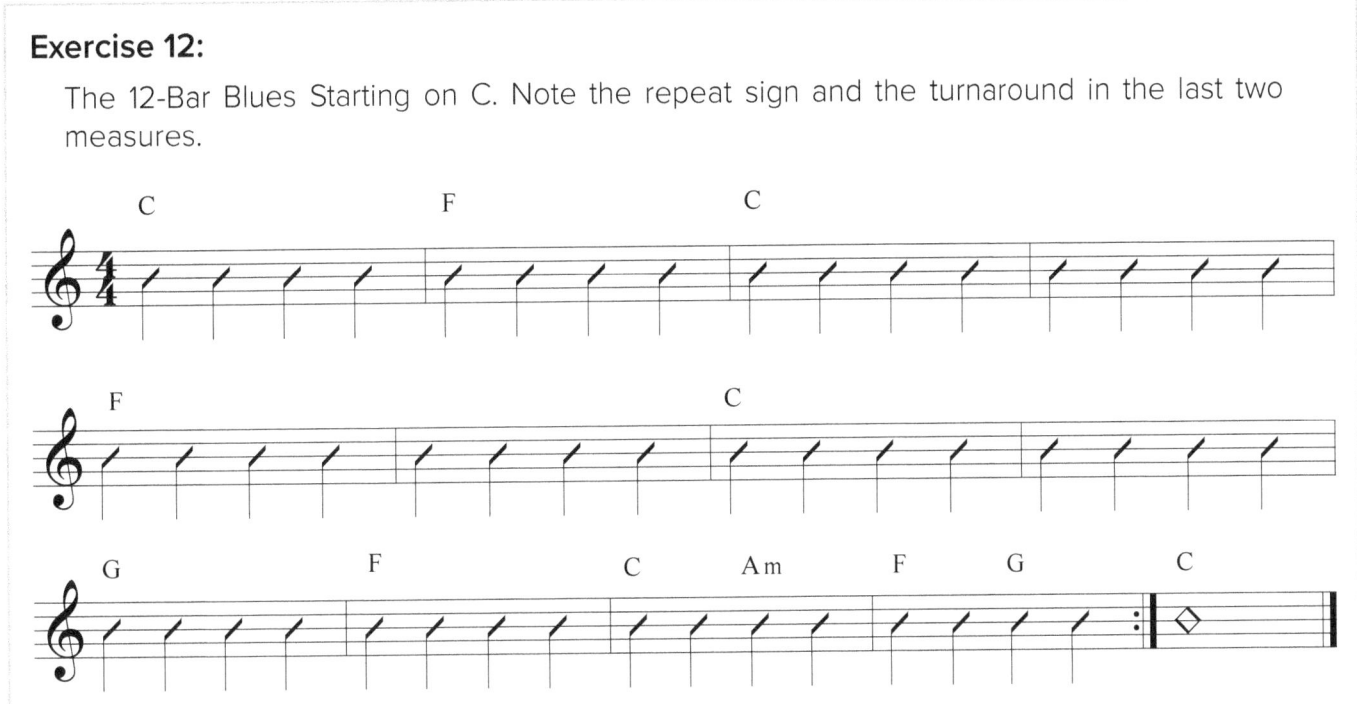

Review:

Play Exercises 6, 7, 8, 9, 10 and the 12-Bar Blues starting on E below.

Exercise 13: The 12-Bar Blues Starting on E.

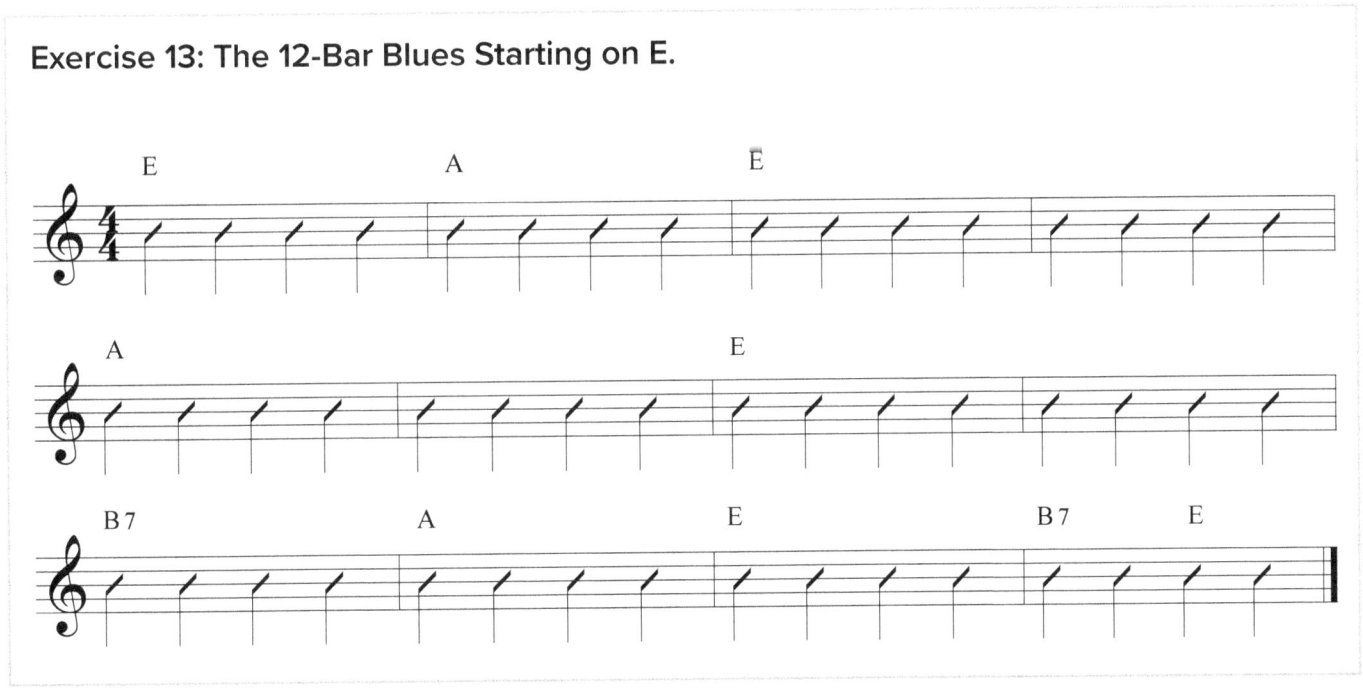

LESSON 5

HOW TO READ TABLATURE

In this lesson, we'll be moving away from learning chords to work on another common method for learning to play the guitar: tablature. Tablature (or TAB) is the most popular way of learning new songs. It is almost as old as standard notation for stringed instruments. The advantages of TAB are that it's easy to read and it allows you to figure out songs much faster than standard notation. However, there are some drawbacks. Perhaps the biggest of these is that most TABS do not include any rhythm, meaning you have to either know how the song is supposed to sound ahead of time or rely on the standard notation, when available.

Tablature shows you *where* to play, while standard notation shows you *what* to play. Therefore, both are equally valuable when learning a new song. (Note: standard notation will be addressed in Lessons 7 and 8.)

To read tablature, first know that each line represents a string on the guitar. The lowest string is the bottom line, and the highest string is the top line (see below). Numbers are placed on the lines to show you on which fret or frets to place your fingers. For example, if you see a number 1 on the first string (the top line), simply play the first fret on the first string. If there is a zero on the line, that means you are to play the string open (without pressing down on a fret).

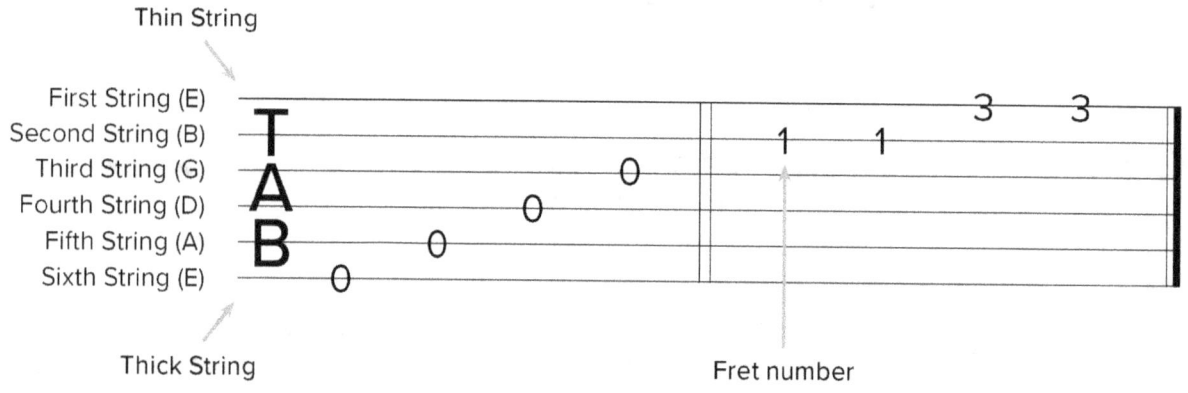

*The fret numbers indicate where to place your fingers.

Try it: Play through the TAB below.

DAY 1 PRACTICE: TAB FOR FAMILIAR TUNES

Warm-Up:

Play Exercise 13 from Lesson 4.

New:

Practice reading TAB using the exercises below.

Exercise 1:

Play the tune to "Twinkle, Twinkle, Little Star"

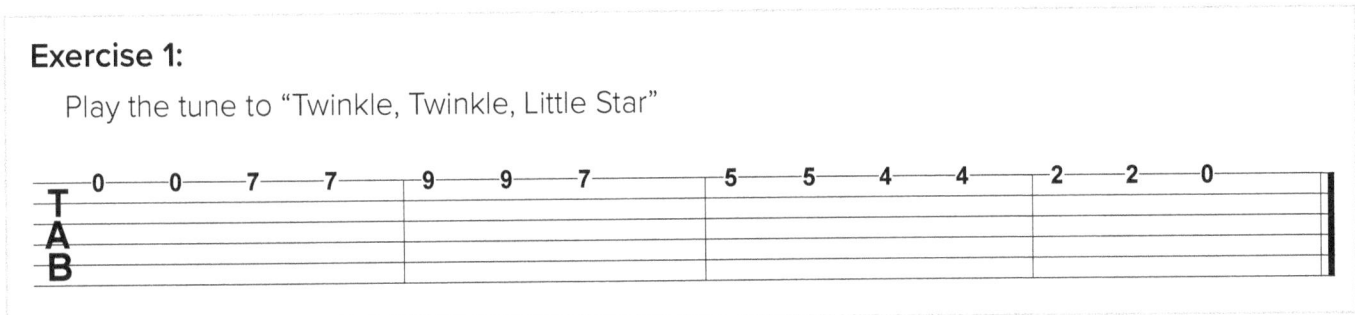

Exercise 2:

Play the tune to "Happy Birthday"

Review:

Play Exercises 11 and 12 from Lesson 4.

DAY 2 PRACTICE: TABLATURE FOR A FULL MELODY

Warm-Up:

Play Exercises 11, 12, and 13 from Lesson 4.

New:

For today's practice, you will be playing a well-known melody from beginning to end. Note that when playing the notes on the first fret, use your first finger; when playing notes on the third fret, use your third finger. When playing single notes, keep your wrist dropped, your fingers on their tips, and press down on the wood section of the fret right next to the metal bar.

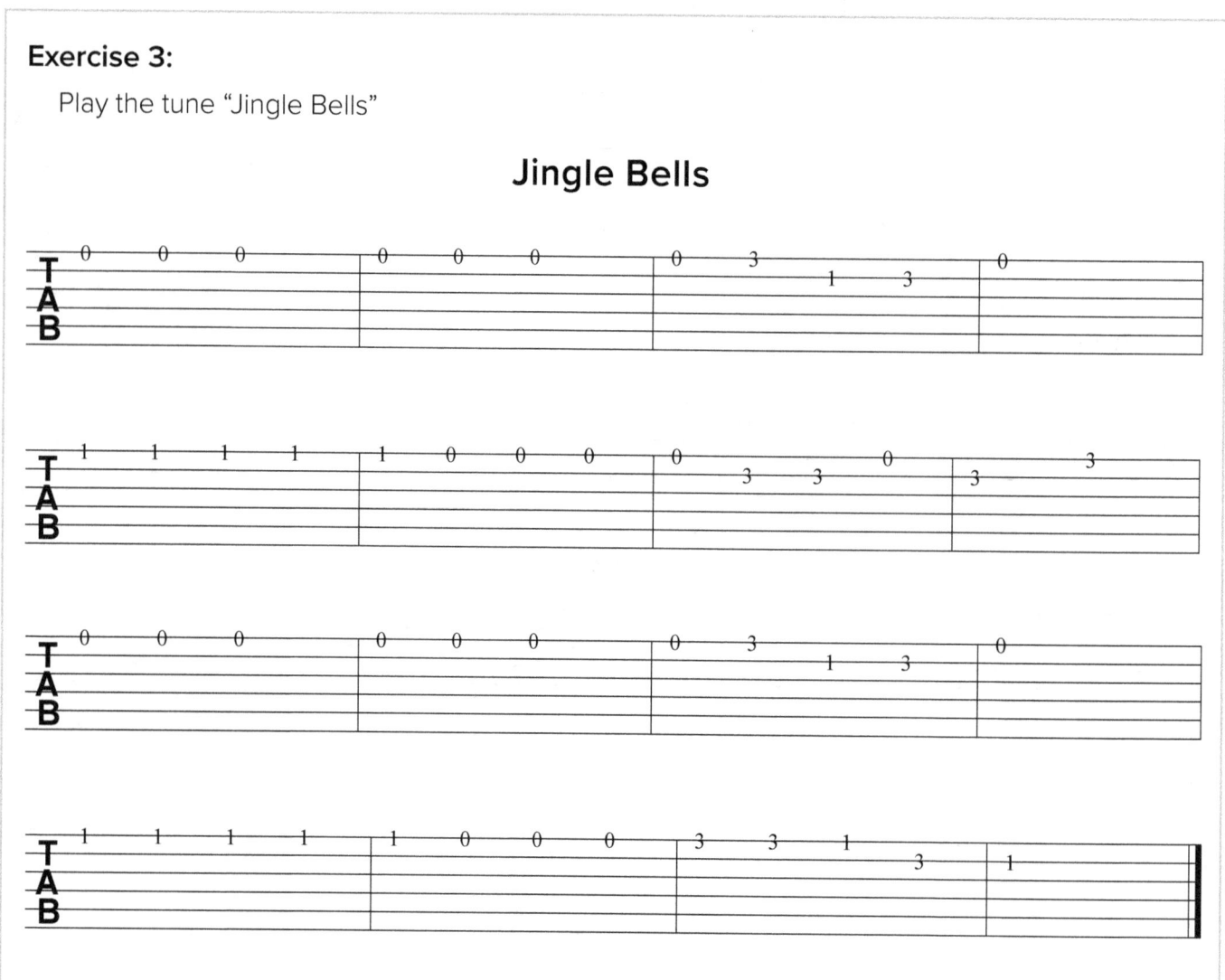

Review:

Play Exercises 1 and 2.

DAY 3 PRACTICE: RIFFS IN TAB

Warm-Up:

Play Exercises 1 and 2.

New:

Today we'll practice reading TABS using riffs. A **riff** is simply a repeated pattern that is used as the accompaniment to a song. Be sure to follow the standard fingerings (see box).

> **Use this fingering:**
>
> First Fret : First Finger
>
> Second Fret: Second Finger
>
> Third Fret: Third Finger
>
> Fourth Fret: Fourth Finger

Exercise 4:

Play the following riff

Unified Storm

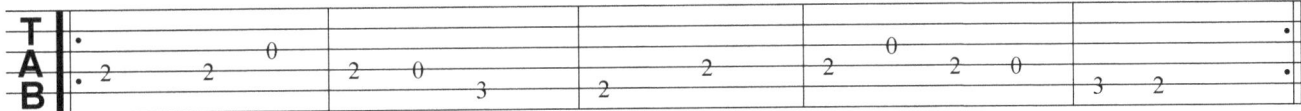

Exercise 5:

Play the following riff

Be Yourself

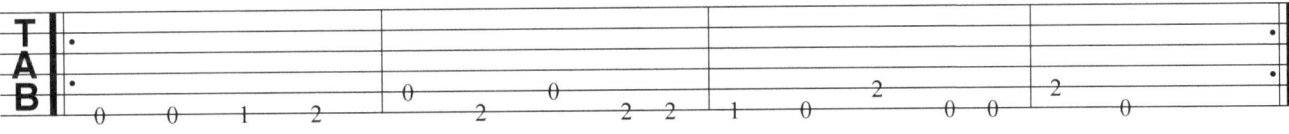

Exercise 6:

Play the following riff

Canned Dinner

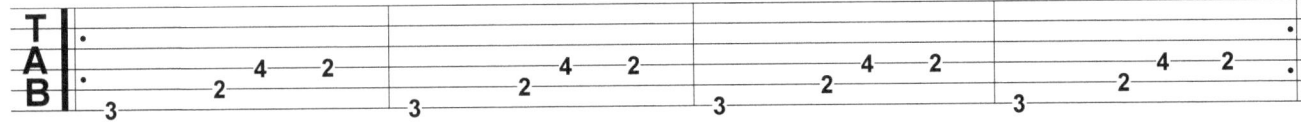

Exercise 7:

Play the following riff

That Girl

Review:

Play Exercise 3

DAY 4 PRACTICE: TWO NOTE TABLATURE

Warm-Up:

Play Exercises 1, 2, and 3.

New:

For today's practice, we'll be reading two notes at the same time in the TABs. To do this, first figure out where each finger goes, play it, and then figure out whatever comes next. Be sure to take your time and work out a fingering that feels comfortable for you. In Exercise 8, for example, play strings three and four open at the same time, then play the third fret on the same strings at the same time. To do this, you can either use two different fingers for each string or one finger for both.

Exercise 8:

Play the following riff.

Fire Water

Exercise 9:

Play the following.

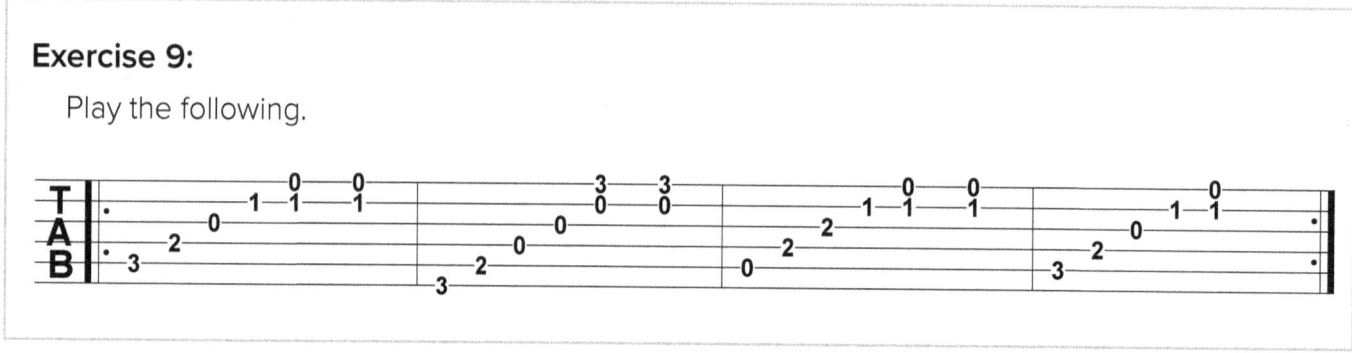

Review:

Play Exercises 4, 5, 6, and 7.

DAY 5 PRACTICE: CHORDS IN TABLATURE

Warm-Up:

Play Exercises 1, 2, and 3.

New:

For today's practice, we'll be reading full chords in TAB form. This can be difficult to do since there is so much information to process when looking at the TAB. However, with time you'll become familiar with many of the most commonly used guitar chord voicings.

To read chords from TAB, start from the lowest note and figure out the chord one note at a time. The chords used in the following exercises are all ones you've played before in this book, so be sure to label them once you've figure them out.

Exercise 10:

Figure out the following chords, and then strum through the exercise.

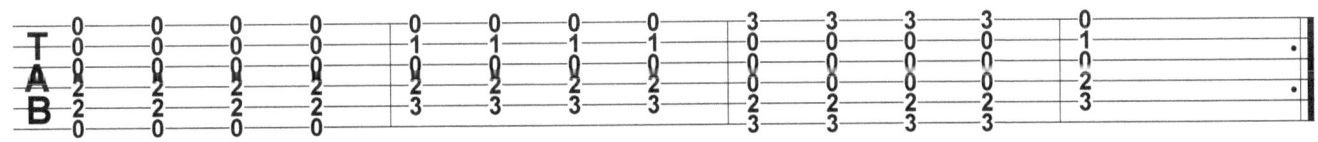

Exercise 11:

Often the chord symbols will be included along with the TAB to help you. In this exercise, the chords are broken up to create a bass/chord accompaniment pattern. First put your fingers down as if you are going to strum the chord. Then play the bass note, which is the lowest note of the chord, indicated in the TAB; then strum the rest of the chord on beat 2 etc.

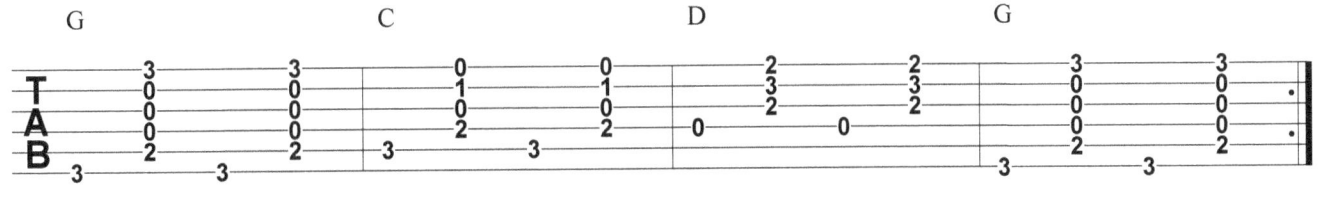

Review:

Play Exercises 4, 5, 6, 7, 8, and 9.

DAY 6 PRACTICE: CHORDS & TAB

Warm-Up:

Play Exercises 1, 2, 3, 4 and 5.

New:

For today's practice, we are going to use one song to practice both chords and TABs. Play either the TAB first or the chords, then go back and play the other. Each is a different part to the same song.

Exercise 12:

First, follow the Guitar 1 part. Figure out the chords, and then strum through the exercise. Second, go back and play the Guitar 2 part using the tablature.

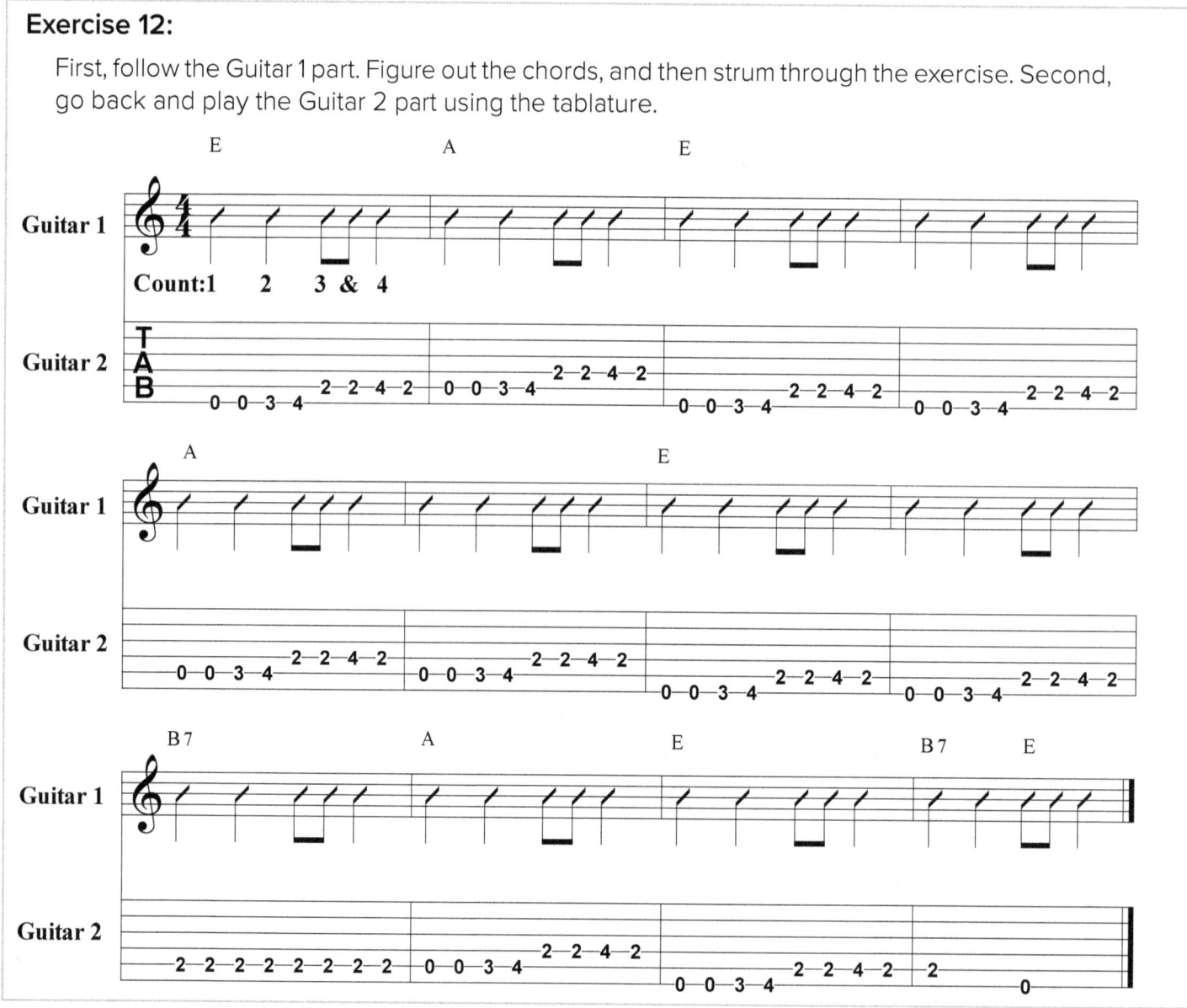

Review:

Play Exercises 6, 7, 8, 9, 10 and 11.

LESSON 6

BUILDING TECHNIQUE WITH WARM-UPS

Now that you've learned chords and TAB, you are ready to start learning warm-up techniques. Learning any instrument comes down to two main factors: (1.) understanding the music and (2.) learning the physical techniques needed in order to be able to produce the sounds you want on the instrument.

Including a dedicated warm-up for each practice session can help you develop this physical technique, and in doing so, it will help you build finger strength, dexterity, and give you a stronger command of your instrument.

We'll begin by developing your fret-hand technique on Practice Days 1-4, and then later in the week work on your picking-hand.

DAY 1 PRACTICE: THE SPIDER WALK

Warm-Up:

Play Exercise 12 from Lesson 5.

New:

For today's practice, you'll learn how to play a common guitar exercise called "The Spider Walk."

To play this:

1. Start on the 5th fret of the 6th string with the 1st finger. Play that note.

2. Then keeping your first finger in place, put your 2nd finger down at the 6th fret, then play it.

3. Keeping both fingers down, play the 7th fret with the 3rd finger. Then play the 8th fret with the 4th finger, while keeping all the other fingers down on the fretboard.

4. Then move through the same notes backwards. Do not play the open string. (See Exercise 1.)

Exercise 1:

Spider Walk Step One

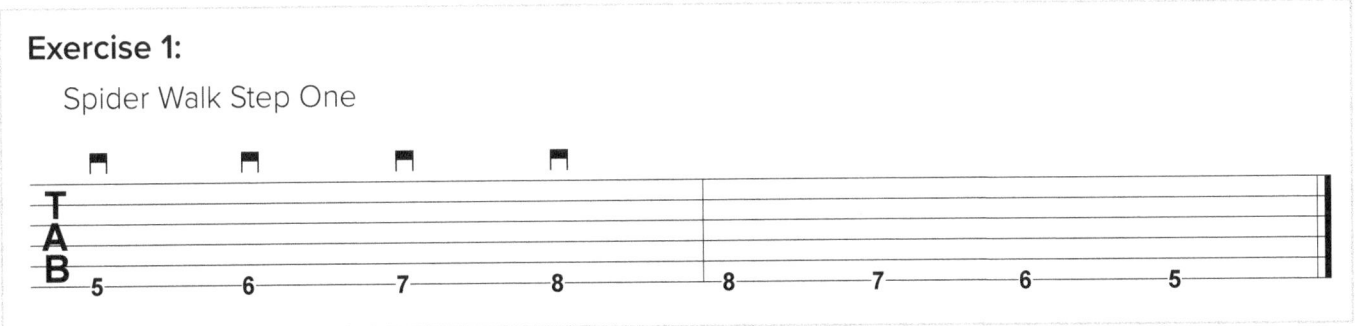

Exercise 2:

Spider Walk Step Two

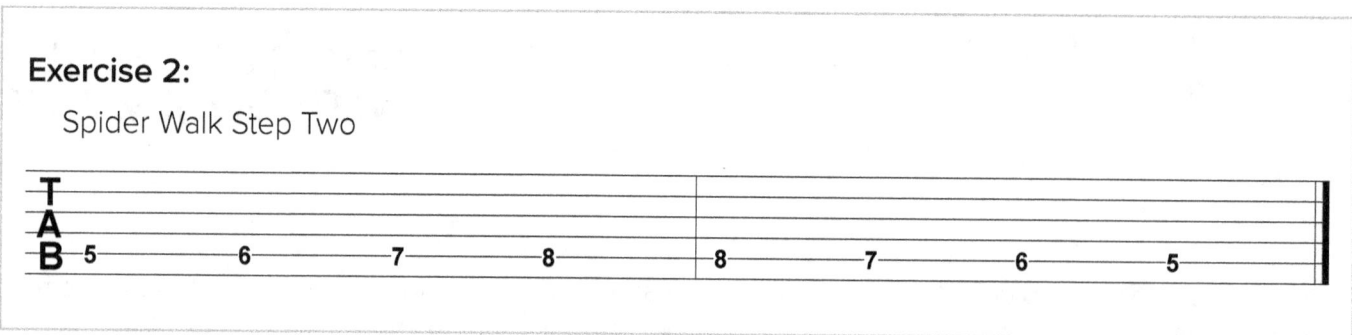

Exercise 3:

Spider Walk Steps One and Two Combined

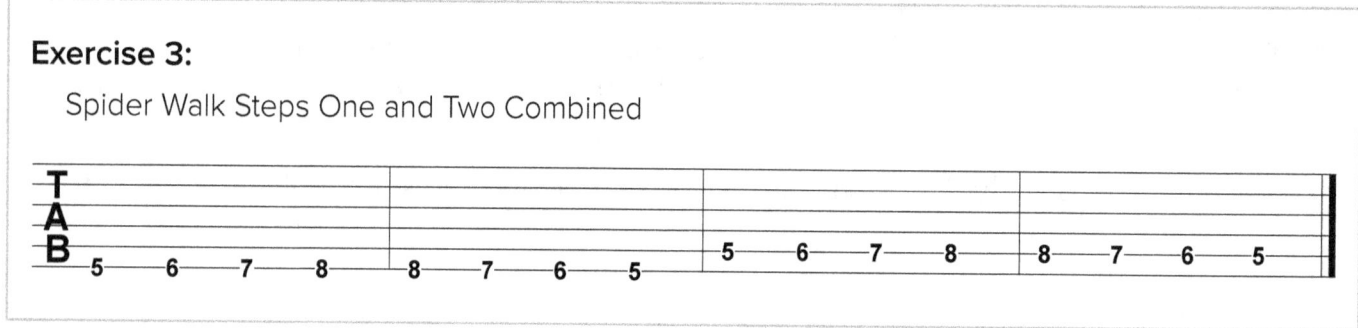

Review:

Play Exercises 10 and 11 from Lesson 5.

DAY 2 PRACTICE: SPIDER WALK 2

Warm-Up:

Play Exercises 8 and 9 from Lesson 5.

New:

For today's practice, we'll continue with the spider walk exercises started on Day 1 Practice. Be sure to keep your fingers down once you put them in place when ascending.

Exercise 4:
Spider Walk Step Three

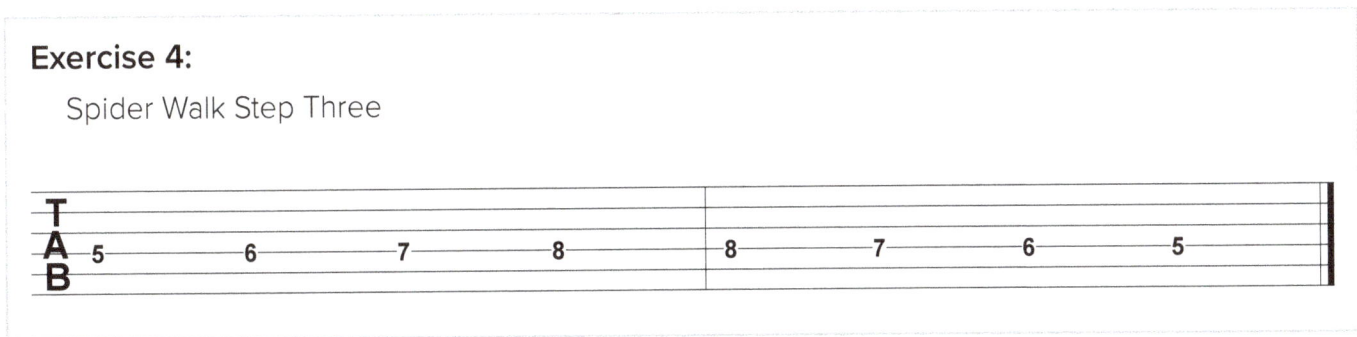

Exercise 5:
Spider Walk Step Four

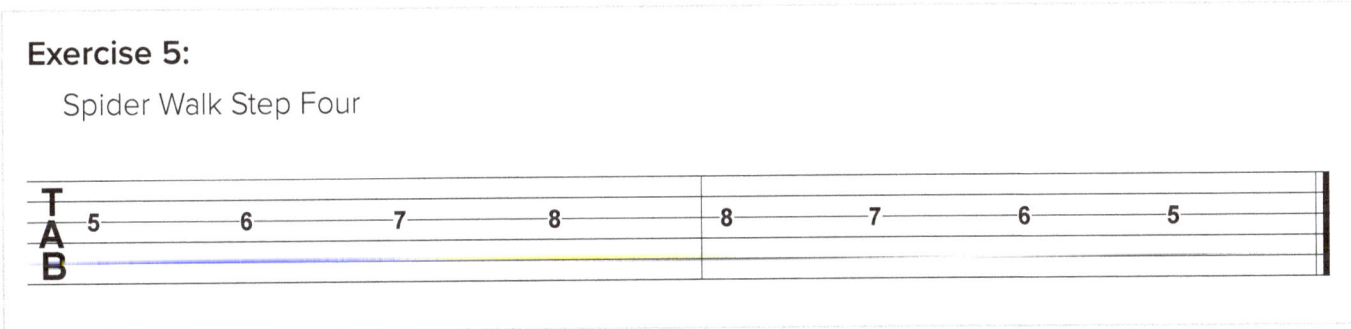

Exercise 6:
Spider Walk Steps Three and Four Combined

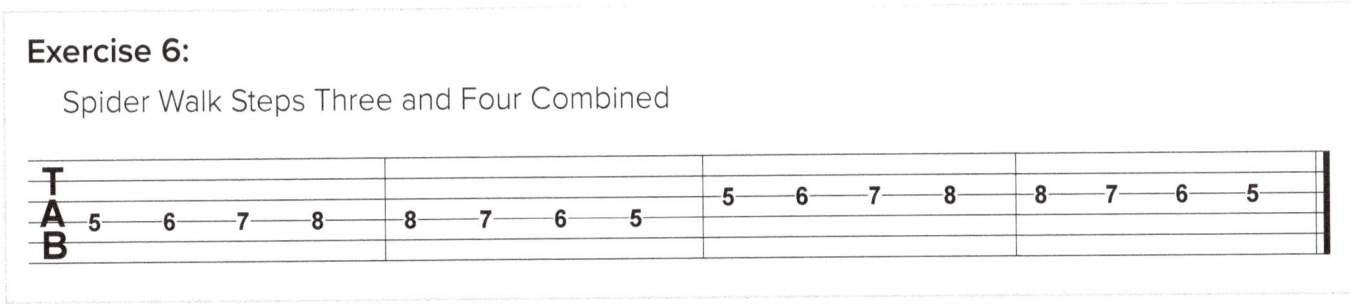

Review:

Play Exercise 3. Then play Exercises 4, 5, 6, and 7 from Lesson 5.

DAY 3 PRACTICE: SPIDER WALK 3

Warm-Up:

Play Exercises 12 and 13 from Lesson 4.

New:

For today's practice, we'll continue with the spider walk exercises from the past two practice days. Again, be sure to keep your fingers down once you put them in place when ascending.

Exercise 7:
Spider Walk Step Five

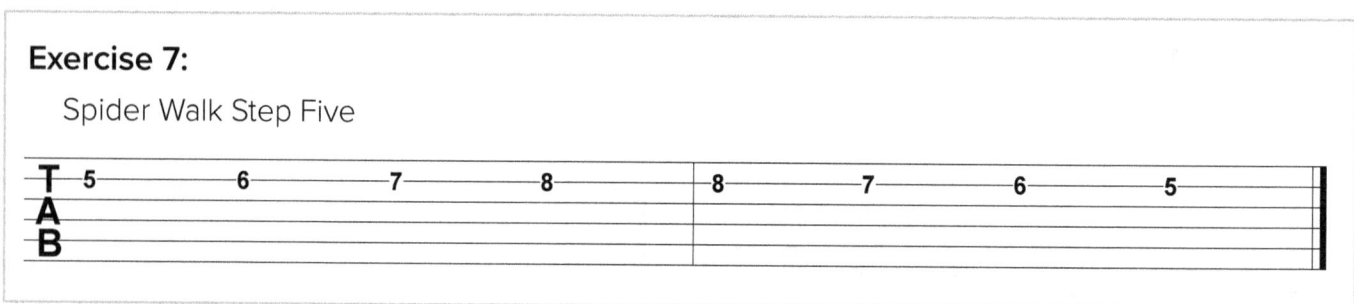

Exercise 8:
Spider Walk Step Six

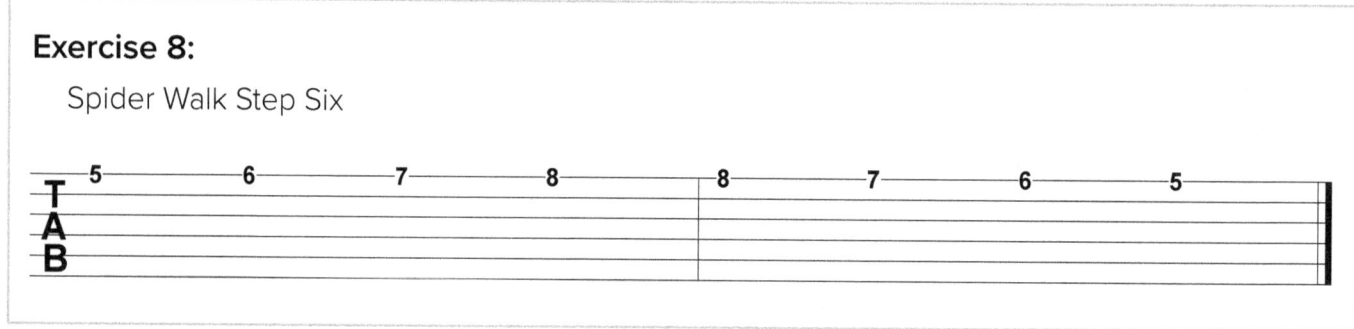

Exercise 9:
Spider Walk Steps Five and Six Combined

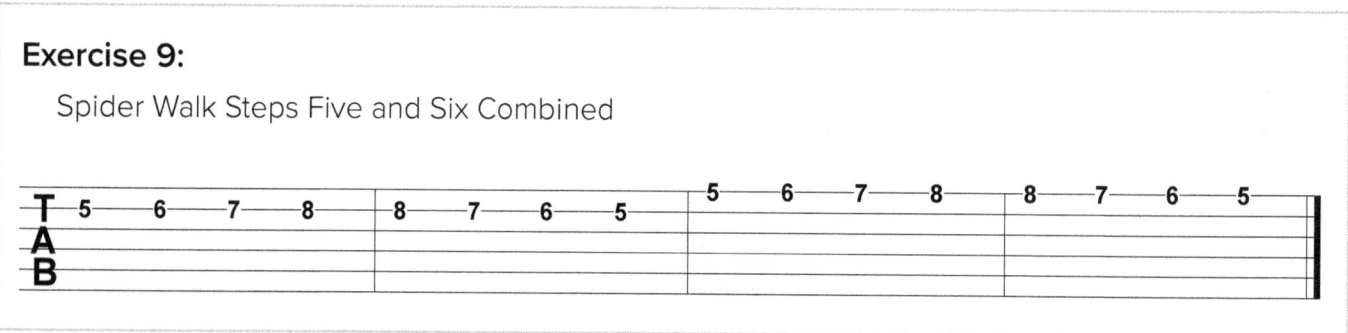

Review:

Play Exercises 3 and 6. Then play Exercises 9 and 10 from Lesson 4.

DAY 4 PRACTICE: THE COMPLETE SPIDER WALK

Warm-Up:

Play Exercise 12 from Lesson 5.

New:

For today's practice, we'll complete the spider walk by putting all the elements together into one complete warm-up exercise.

Exercise 10:

The Complete Spider Walk

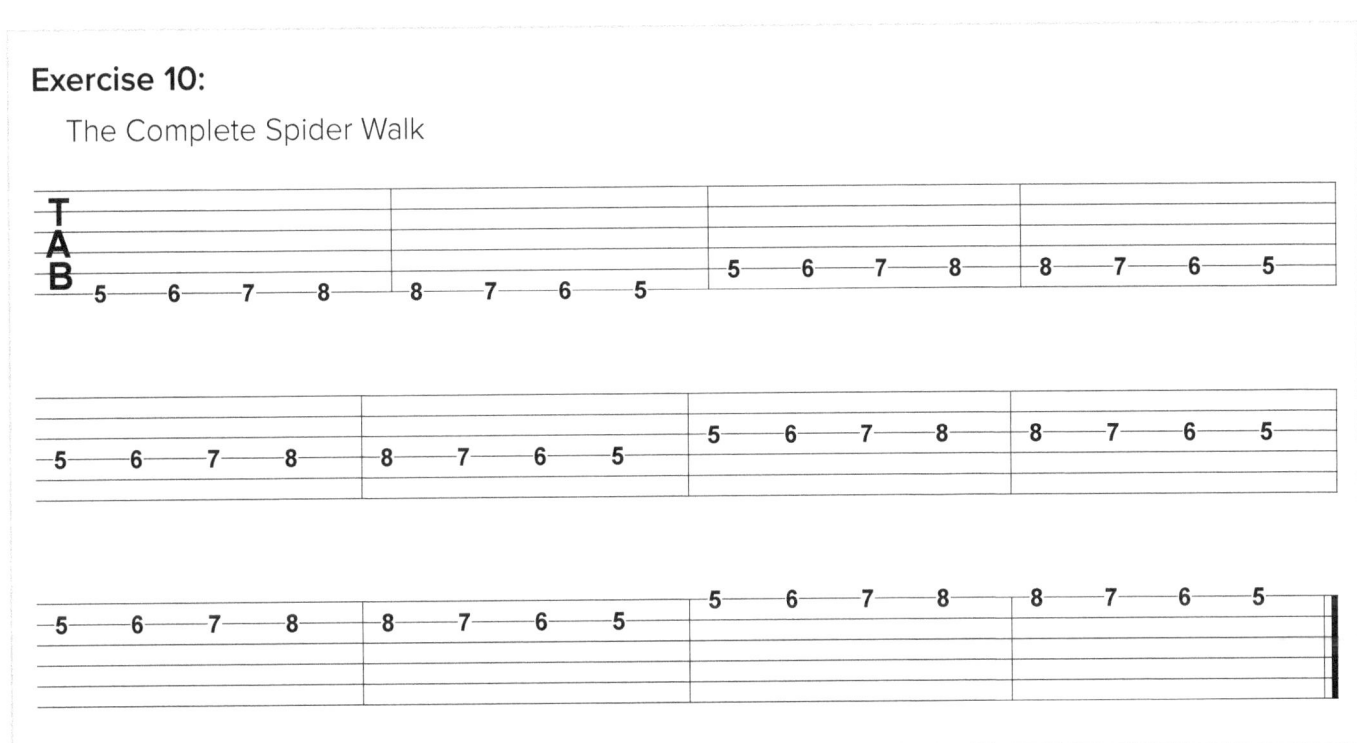

Review:

Play Exercises 3, 4, 5, and 6 from Lesson 5.

DAY 5 PRACTICE: ALTERNATE PICKING THE SPIDER WALK

Warm-Up:

Exercises 3, 6, and 9.

New:

For today's practice, we'll change our focus to the picking-hand. The fret-hand will play a variation on the spider walk, but this time, you'll be using alternate picking. Alternate picking simply means that you'll pick down and then up.

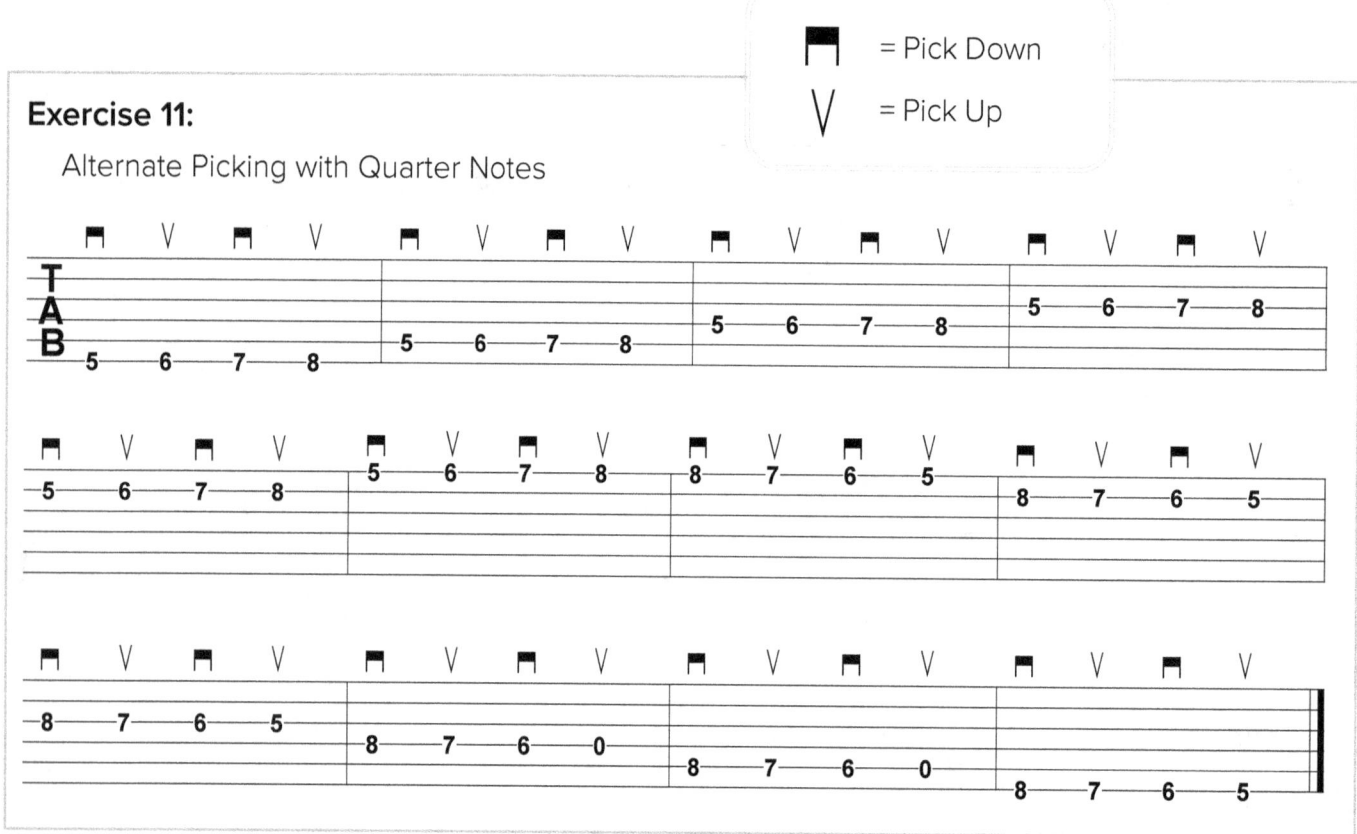

Exercise 11:

Alternate Picking with Quarter Notes

Review:

Exercise 10.

DAY 6 PRACTICE: ALTERNATE PICKING WITH EIGHTH NOTES

Warm-Up:

Exercises 3, 6, and 9.

New:

For today's practice, we'll play the same thing as Exercise 11, but this time we'll be using eighth note rhythms, alternating down on the beat, and up on the "ands" or off-beats.

Exercise 12:

Alternate Picking with Eighth Notes

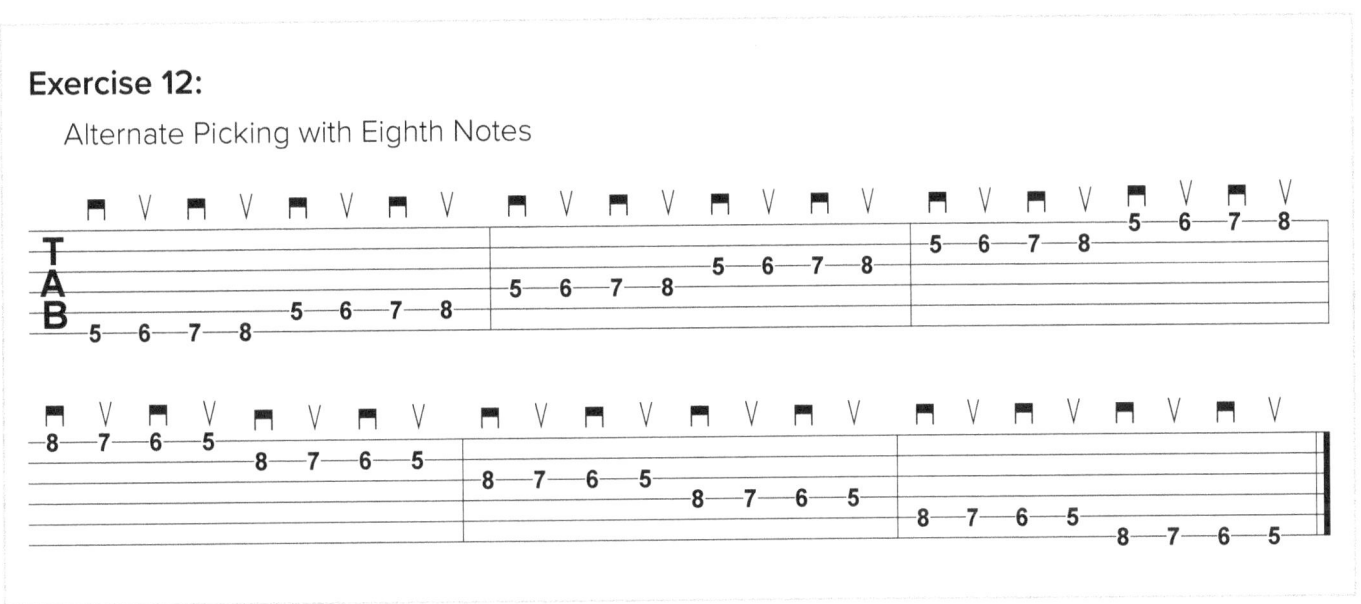

Review:

- Exercises 10 and 11.
- From Lesson 4, review Exercises 9 and 10.
- From Lesson 5, review both parts of Exercise 12.

LESSON 7

HOW TO READ STANDARD MUSICAL NOTATION

In this lesson, you'll be learning how to read music as it pertains to the guitar. Once you understand the basics, you'll be practicing these new skills by learning to read the notes in open position on strings 1-3.

THE ELEMENTS OF READING MUSIC

Understanding Pitch

Pitch simply refers to the highness or lowness of a specific frequency. A **frequency** is how many times a string vibrates per second. For example, the pitch "A" vibrates 440 times per second. (This "A" is found on the first string, fifth fret.) In music, to show what pitch you are to play, noteheads (the dots) are placed on a staff. These dots are more specific than the slash notation used with chords earlier in the book.

The Staff

There are a total of 12 notes that can occur at different pitch levels. Seven of the sounds are given a letter name: A B C D E F G. The remaining five notes fall in between these and will be discussed in a later lesson.

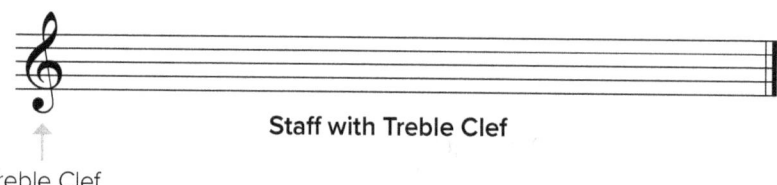

Staff with Treble Clef

Treble Clef

Notes on the Treble Clef

The treble clef tells you what specific notes, or pitches, you can expect to find on its lines and spaces. The lines are (from low to high) E G B D F. The spaces are F A C E. Many elementary schools teach a mnemonic device to help you remember these note names: Every Good Boy Does Fine. And of course the spaces spell FACE.

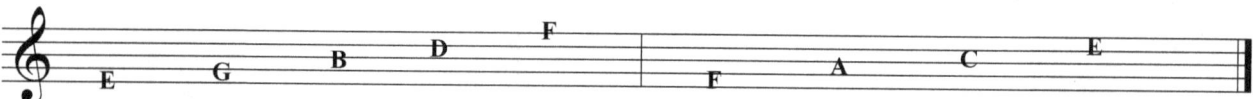

Understanding Time

Time works the same with notation as it does with chords (from Lesson 1). However, instead of slash notation, traditional notation is used. See below.

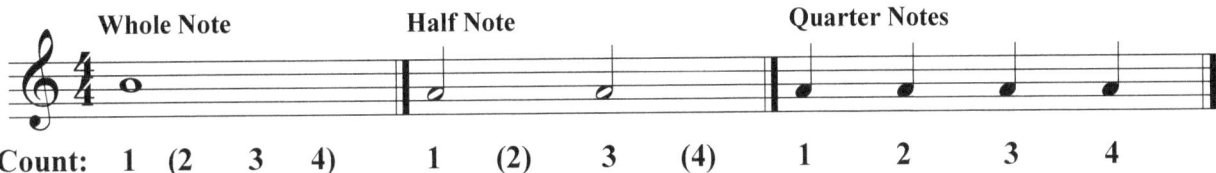

Eighth Notes

Just like with chord strums, a quarter note can be further broken down into two eighth notes, each representing half a beat. When performing eighth notes, pick down on the downbeat, and up on the second half of each eighth note pair, just like Exercise 12 from Lesson 6.

DAY 1 PRACTICE: NOTES ON THE FIRST STRING

Warm-Up:

Play Exercise 10 from Lesson 6.

New:

For today's practice, you'll start learning how to read the notes on the first string in open position. That means you'll be learning the notes E, F, and G and practicing them with a variety of rhythms. TAB has been included on the first three exercises to help you. However, don't rely on it. Only use it as a reference.

Exercise 1:

Play the E note on the first string open. (Open means with no fingers).

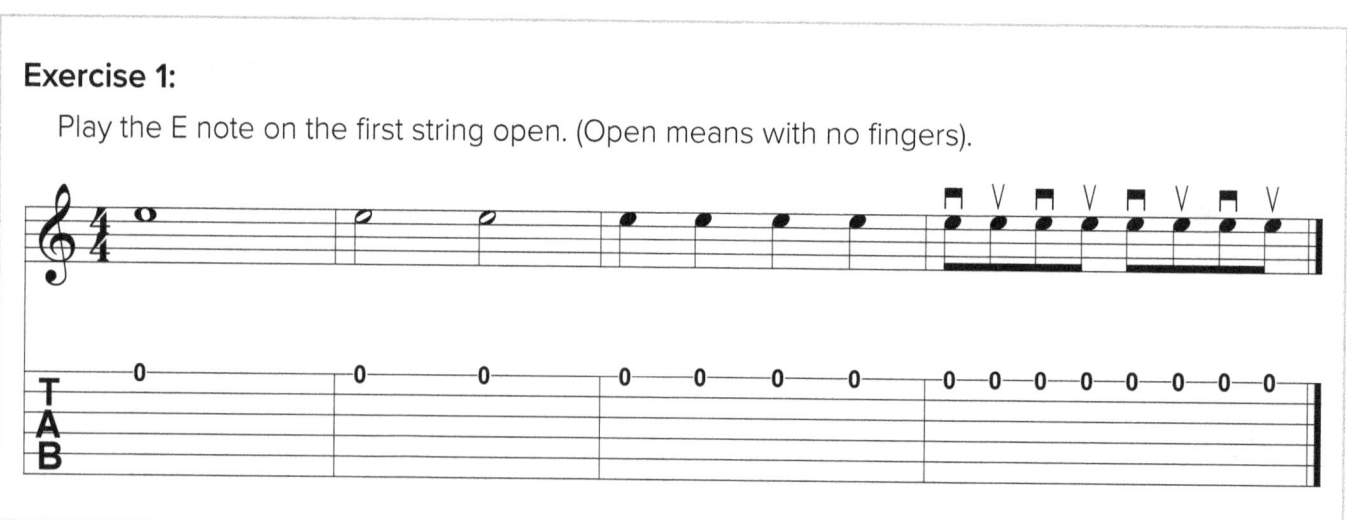

Exercise 2:

Play the F note on the first string, first fret with the first finger.

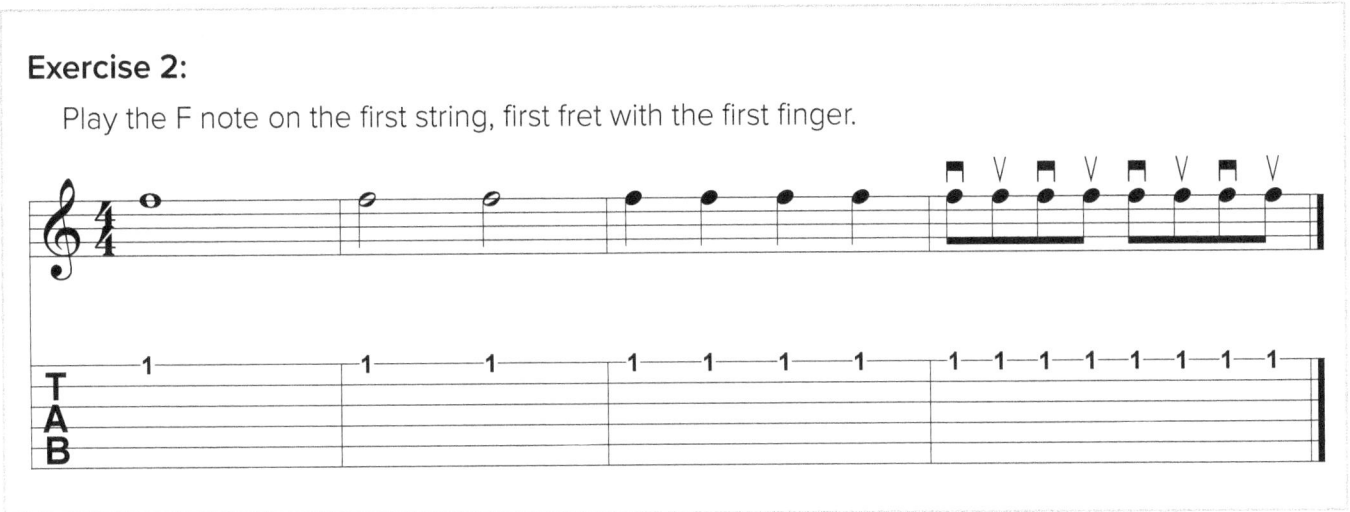

Exercise 3:

Play the G note on the first string, third fret with the third finger.

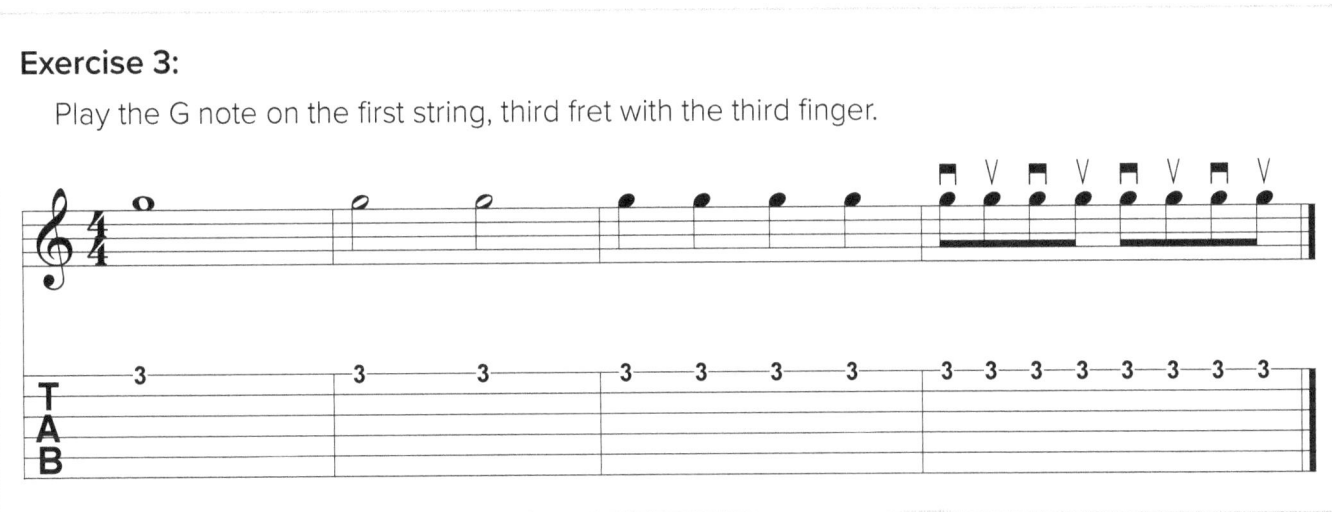

Exercise 4:

Play all three notes without the assistance of TAB.

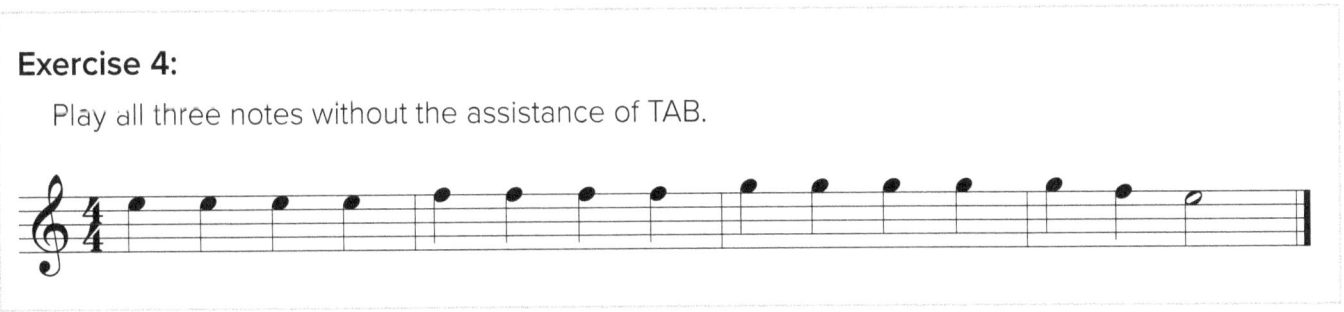

Review:

Play Exercises 6 and 7 from Lesson 4.

DAY 2 PRACTICE: MELODY ON THE FIRST STRING

Warm-Up:

Play Exercise 11 from Lesson 6 and Exercise 4 from Lesson 7.

New:

For today's practice, you'll practice reading the notes on the first string without tablature.

Exercise 5:

Practice all three notes without the assistance of TAB.

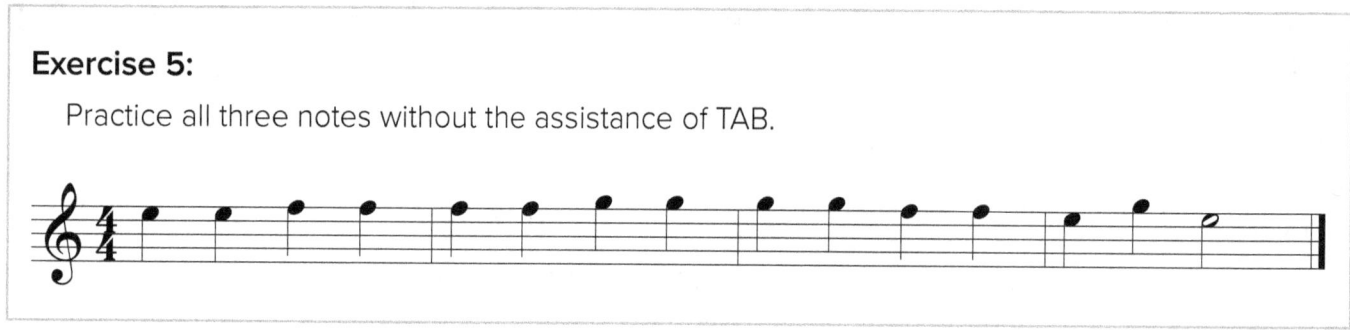

Exercise 6:

Practice this melody.

Rain Drops

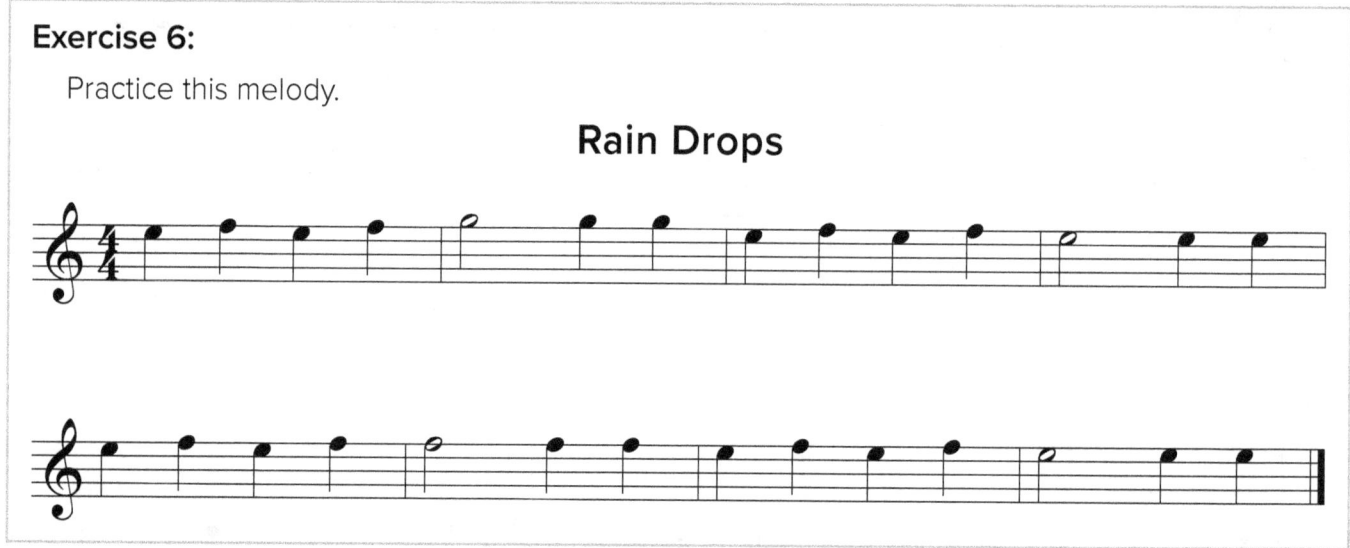

Review:

Play Exercises 1-4. Then play Exercise 11 from Lesson 4.

DAY 3 PRACTICE: NOTES ON THE SECOND STRING

New:

For today's practice, you'll learn the notes B, C, and D on the second string.

Exercise 7:

Play the B note on the second string open.

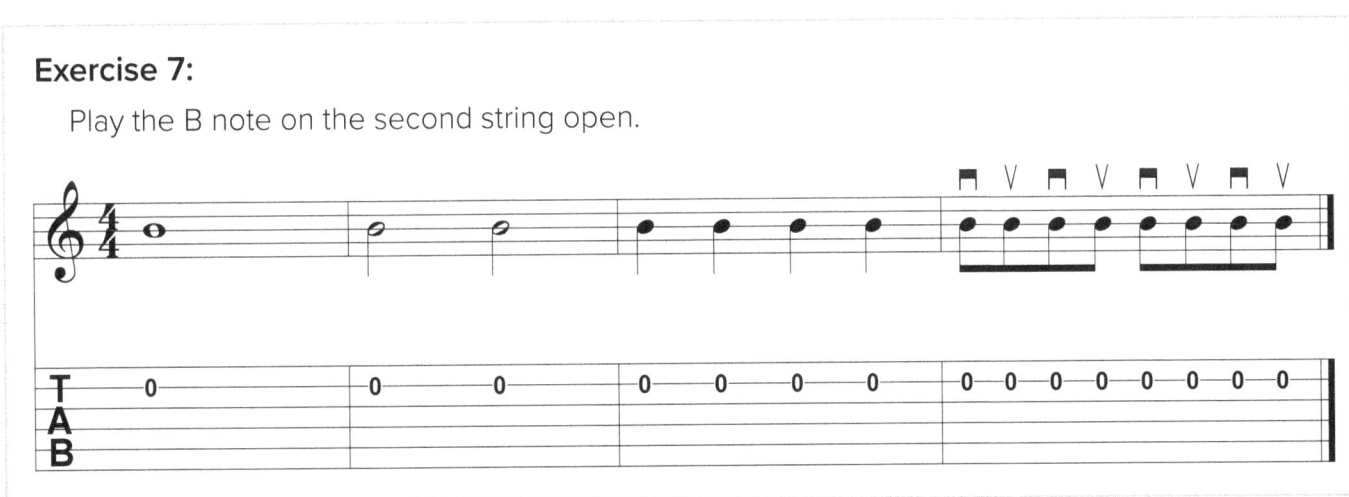

Exercise 8:

Play the C note on the second string, first fret with the first finger.

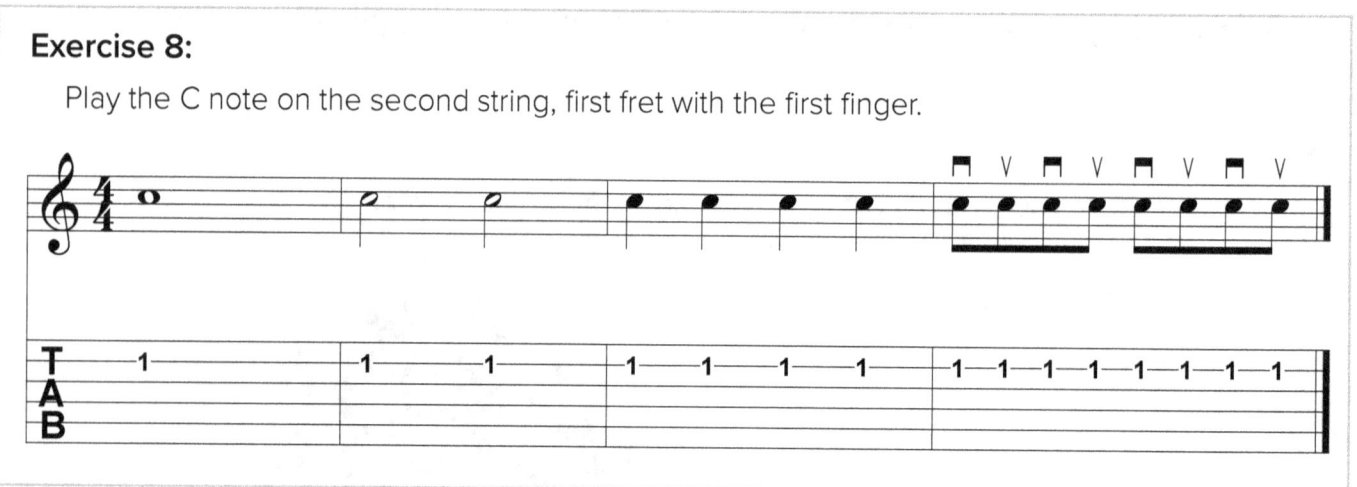

Exercise 9:

Play the D note on the second string, third fret with the third finger.

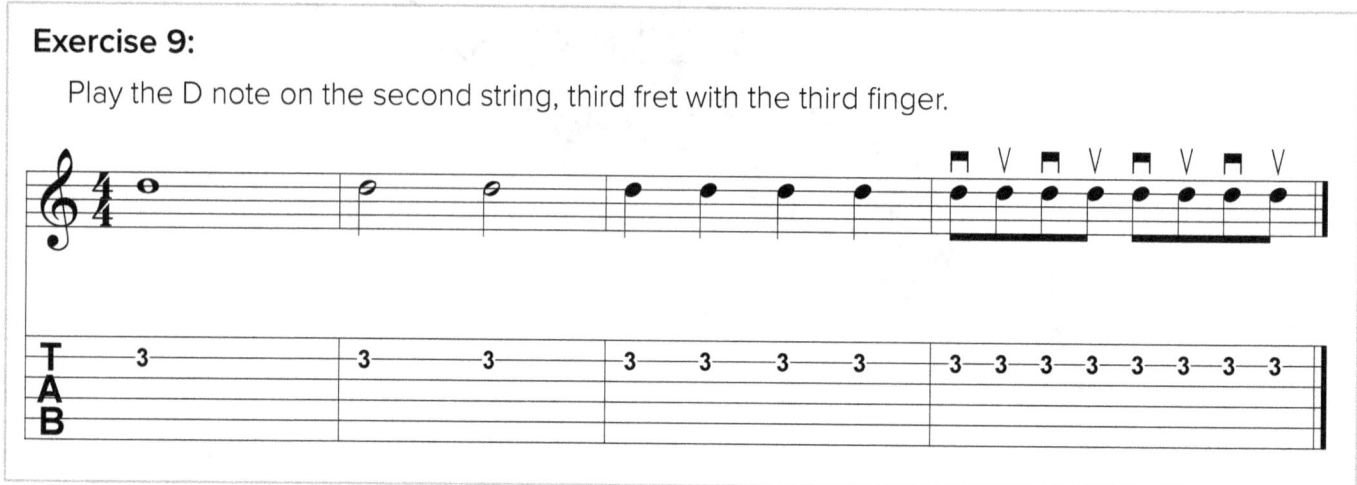

Exercise 10:

Play this melody using all three notes of the second string without TAB.

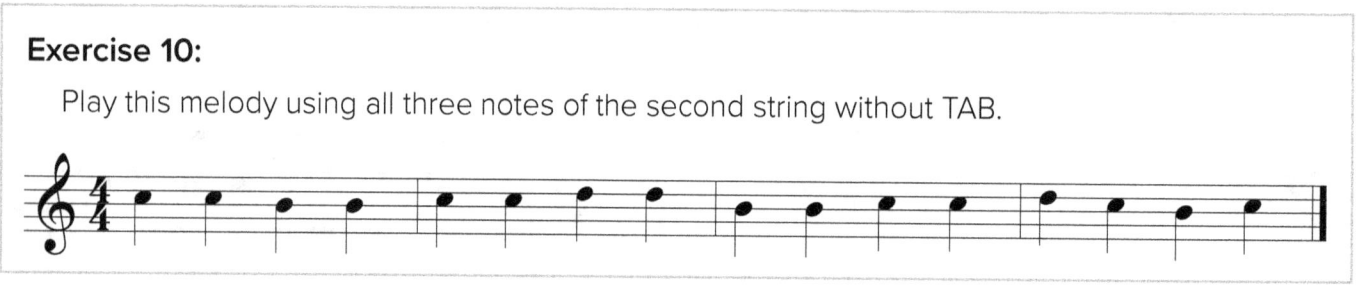

Review:

Play the review Exercise, "Ode to Joy" (Exercise 11), which combines both strings. Use the TAB only as a reference. Then play Exercises 1-4.

Exercise 11:

Play this melody using notes from both strings.

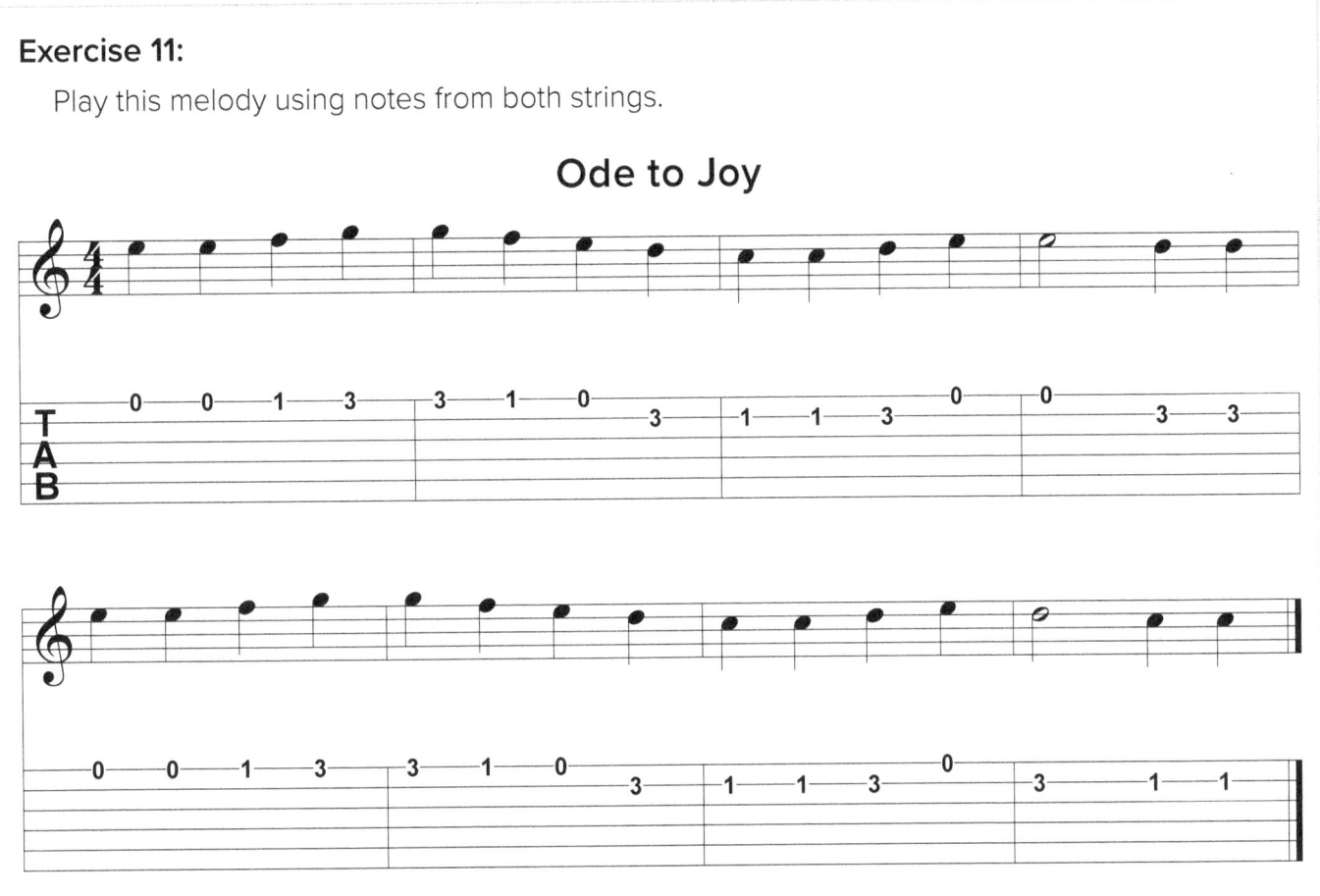

DAY 4 PRACTICE: MELODIES ON TWO STRINGS

Warm-Up:

Play Exercise 12 from Lesson 6.

New:

For today's practice, you'll practice reading the notes on strings one and two.

Exercise 12:

Play this melody using notes from both strings. (This time without the TAB).

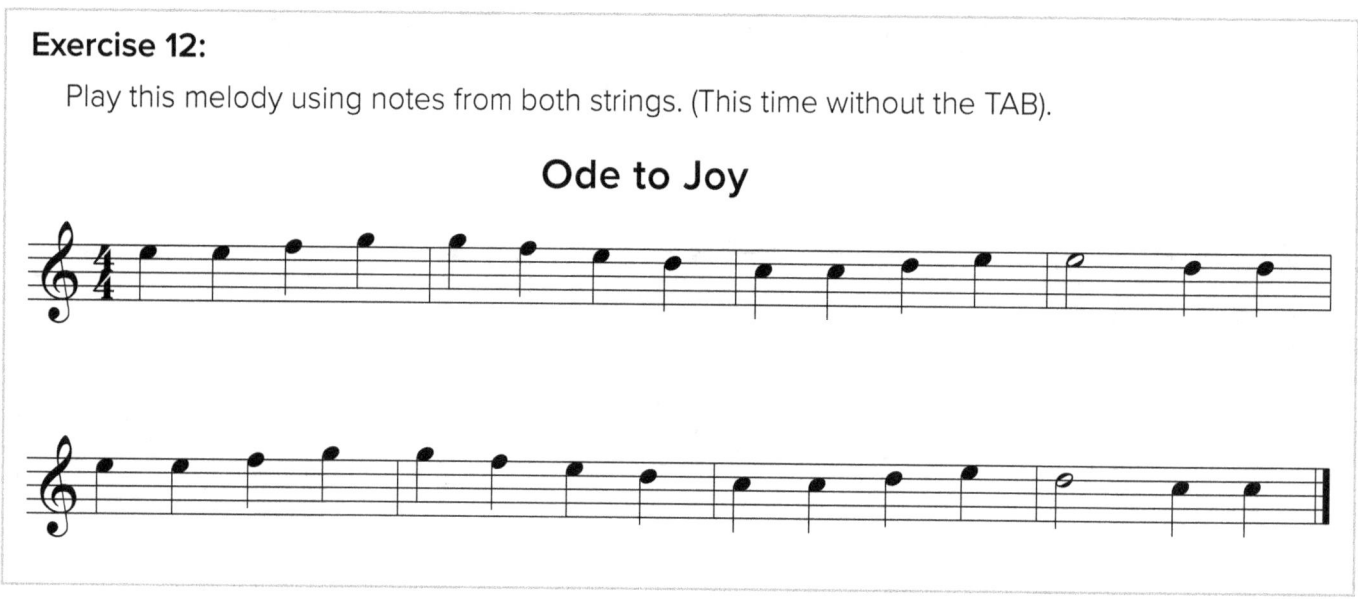

Exercise 13:

Play this melody using notes from both strings.

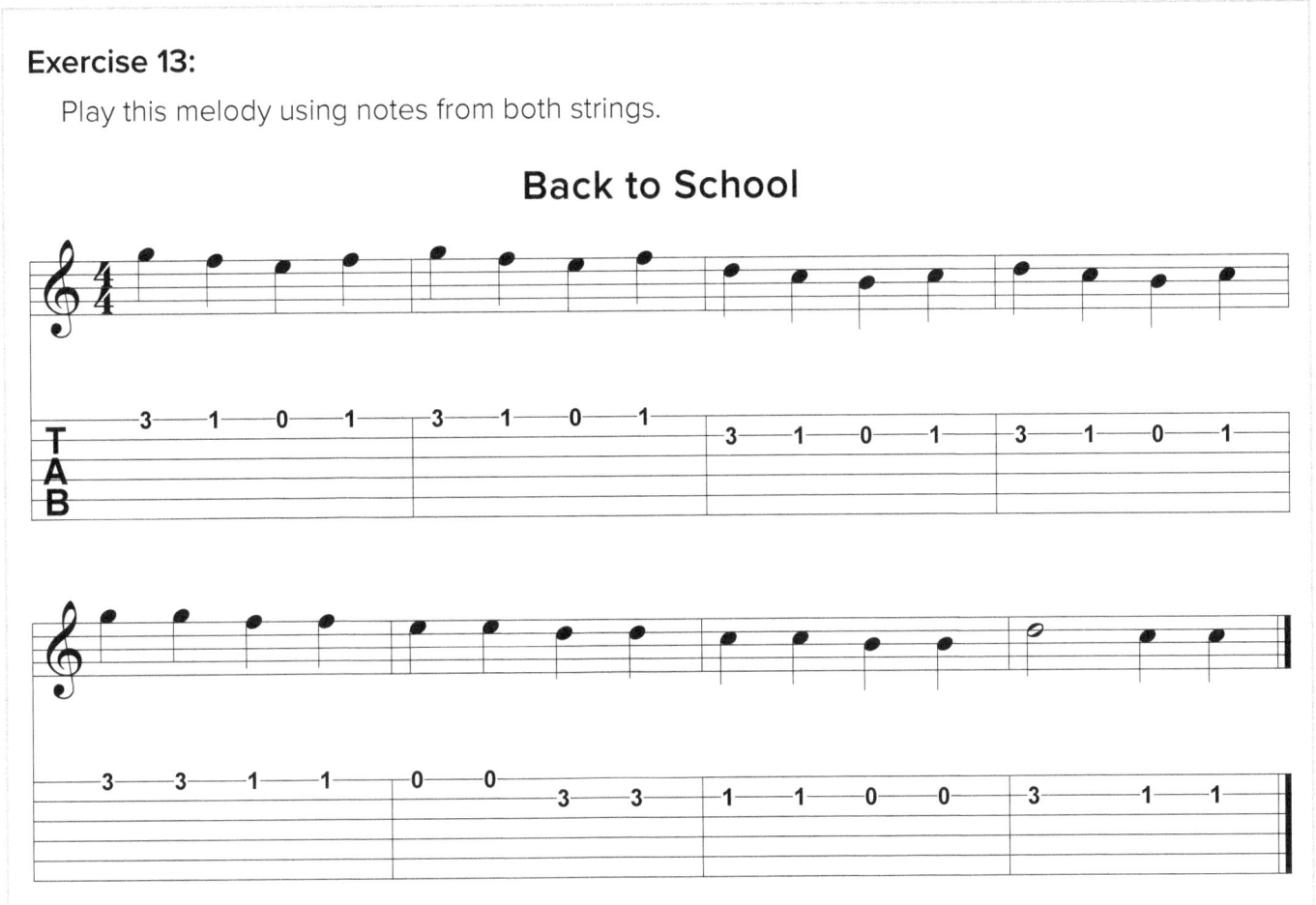

Review:

Play Exercises 4, 5, and 6.

DAY 5 PRACTICE: NOTES ON THE THIRD STRING

Warm-Up:

Play Exercise 11 from Lesson 6.

New:

For today's practice, you'll learn the notes G and A on the third string.

Exercise 14:

Play the new (lower) G note on the third string open.

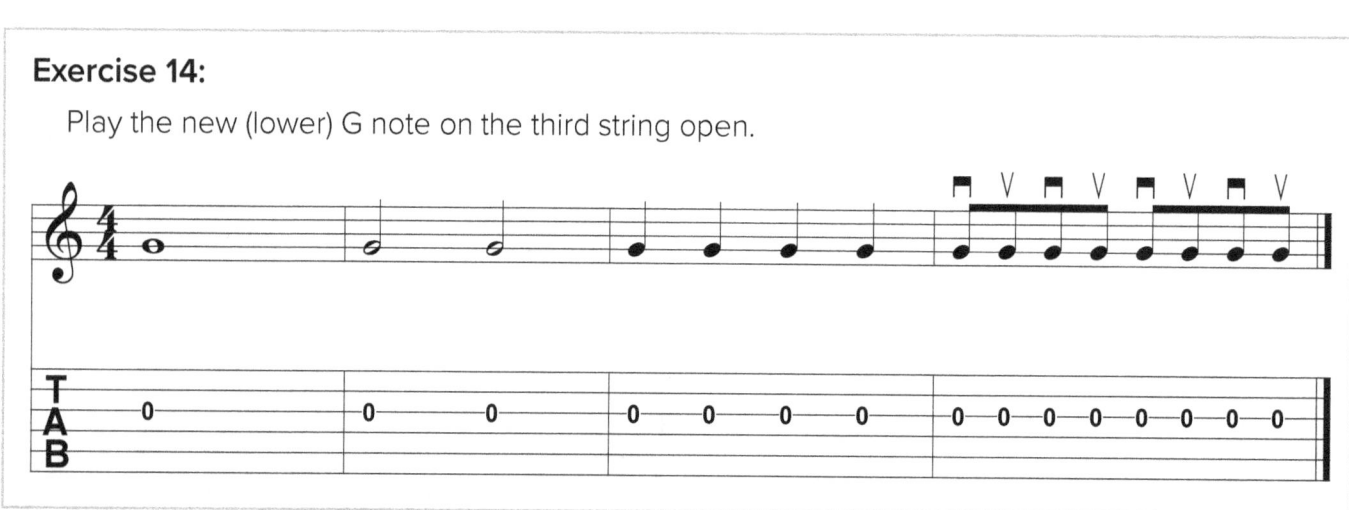

Exercise 15:

Play the A note on the third string, second fret, with the second finger.

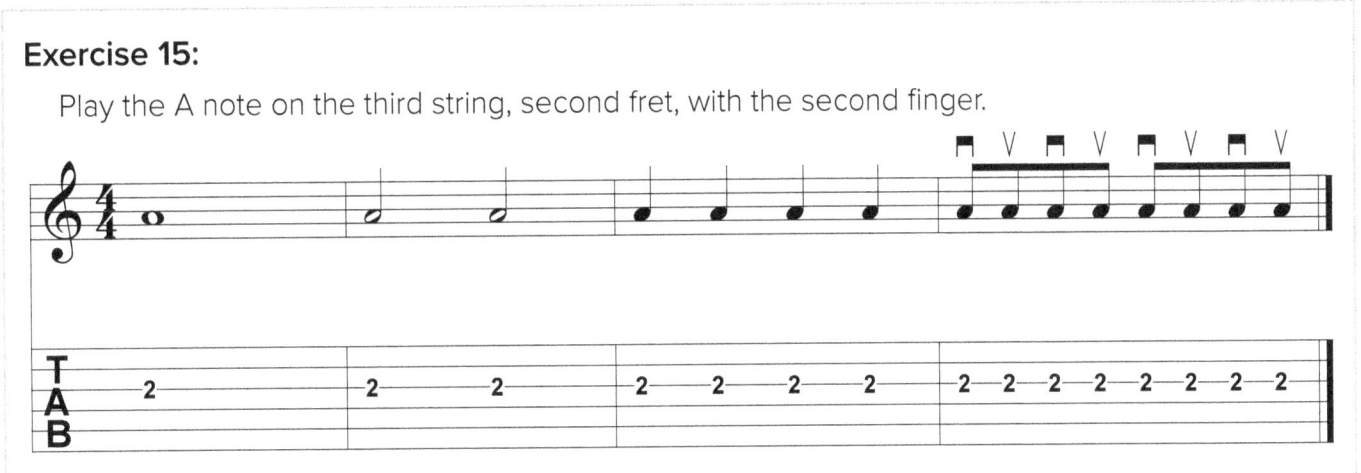

Exercise 16:

Play this melody using the third string notes without TAB.

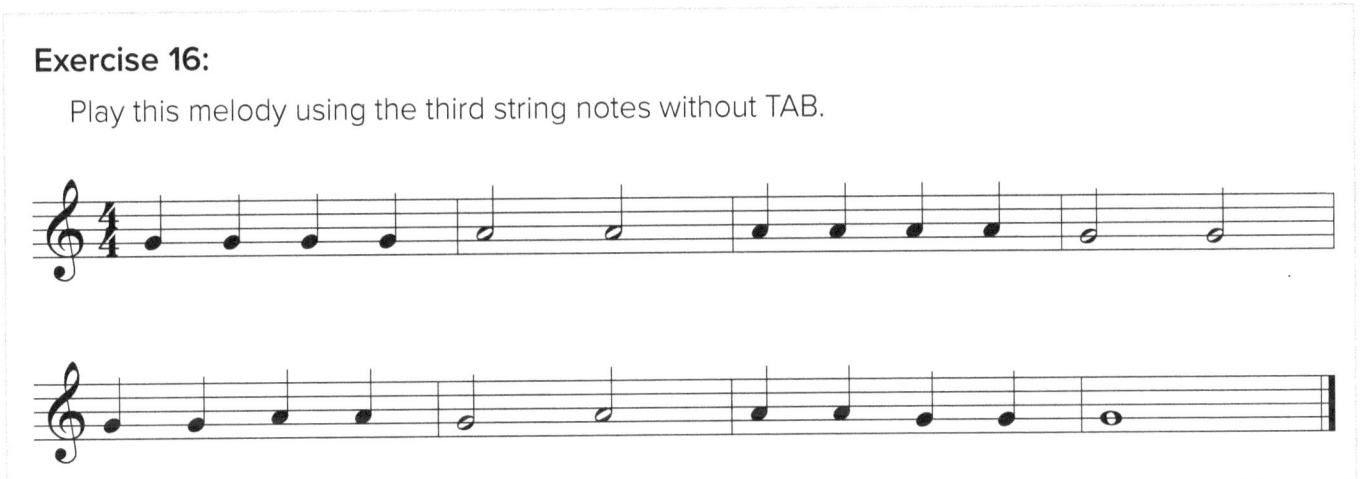

Review:

Play Exercises 4, 5, 6, 12, and 13.

DAY 6 PRACTICE: NOTES ON ALL THREE STRINGS

Warm-Up:

Play Exercise 12 from Lesson 6.

New:

For today's practice, you'll review the notes from all three strings so far.

Exercise 17:

Play this melody using notes from all three strings.

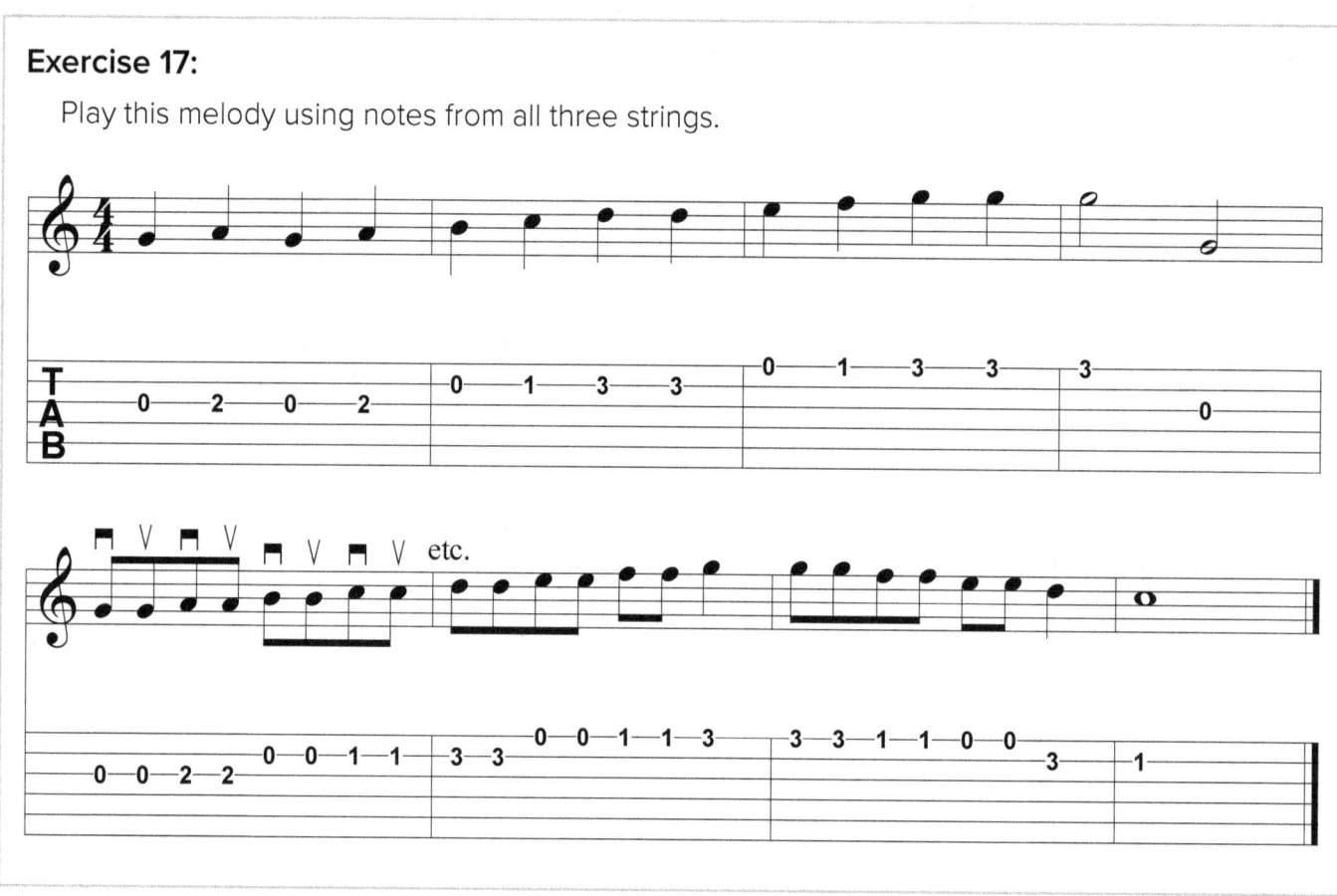

Exercise 18:

Play the following melody, "Three String Blues," using all three strings without TAB.

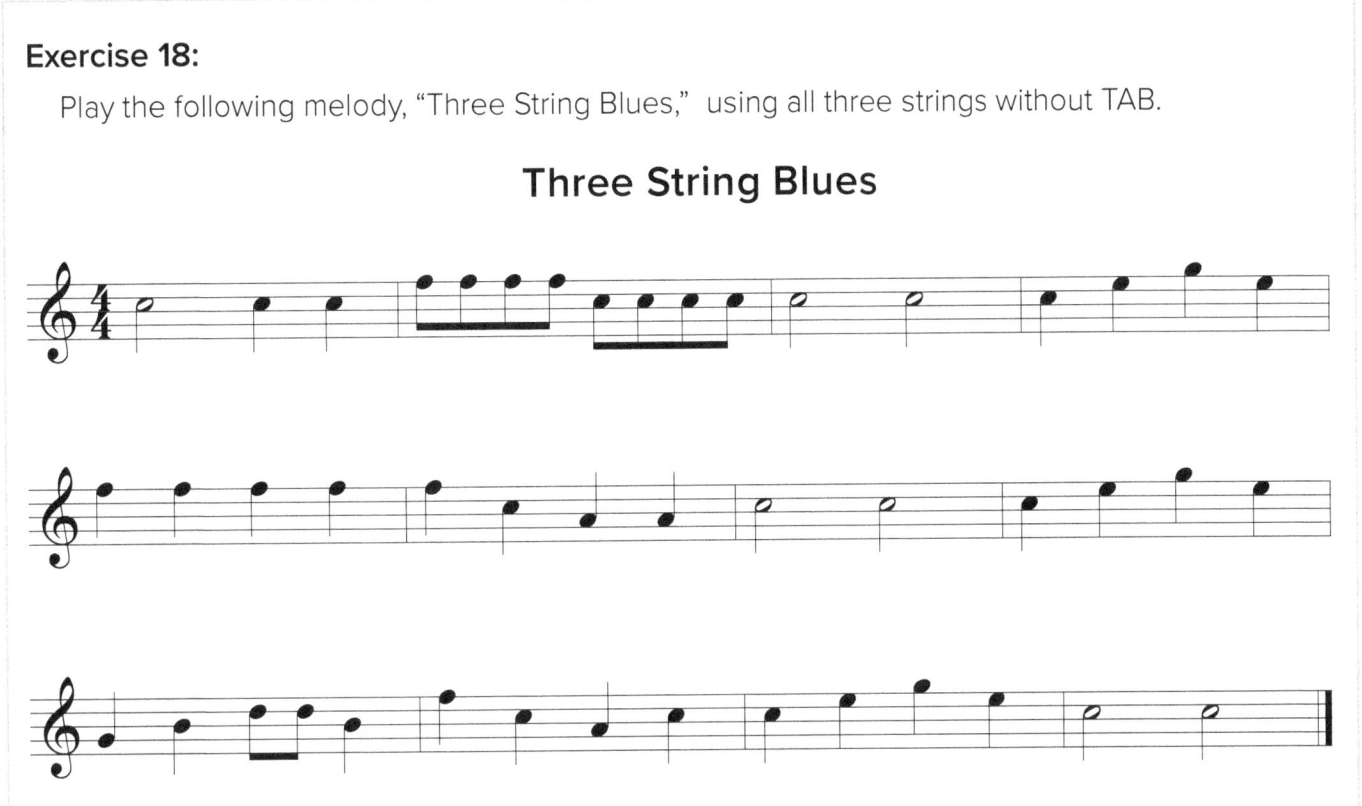

Review:

Play the Exercise below while saying the note names aloud.

Exercise 19:

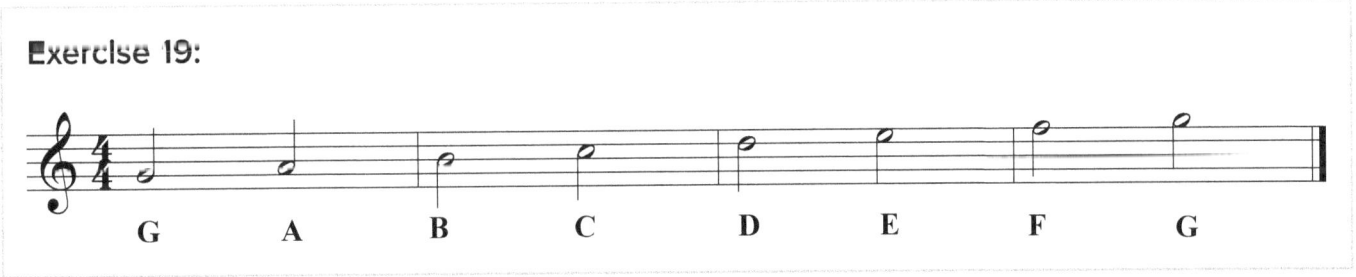

LESSON 8

NOTE READING ON STRINGS 4-6

In this lesson, you'll be continuing to learn how to read standard notation, focusing on strings 4, 5, and 6.

MORE ELEMENTS OF READING MUSIC

Ledger Lines

It is possible to go higher and lower than what is on the staff. When this is done, the extra notes are placed on lines called **ledger lines** (see below).

Ledger Lines

Octaves

In Lesson 7, you learned two different "G" notes, one on the first string, third fret, and the other as the open third string. These two notes are the same pitch, but one is higher than the other. If you count the number of notes between the low G and the high G (G A B C D E F G) you'll get eight notes. This eight note distance is called an **octave.**

In this lesson, many of the notes found on strings 4, 5, and 6 are one or more octaves from the notes you learned in Lesson 7.

Example Octave (G to G)

DAY 1 PRACTICE: NOTES ON THE FOURTH STRING

Warm-Up:

Play Exercise 10 from Lesson 6.

New:

For today's practice, you'll start learning how to read the notes D, E, and F on string 4 in open position.

Exercise 1:

Play the D note on the fourth string open.

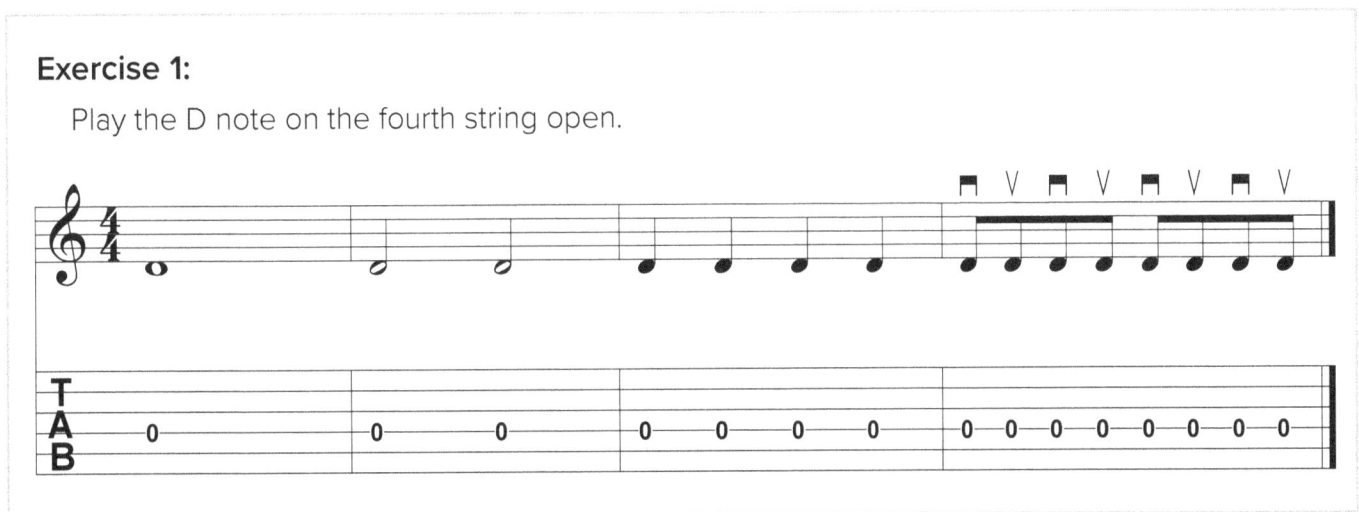

Exercise 2:
Play the E note on the fourth string, second fret with the second finger.

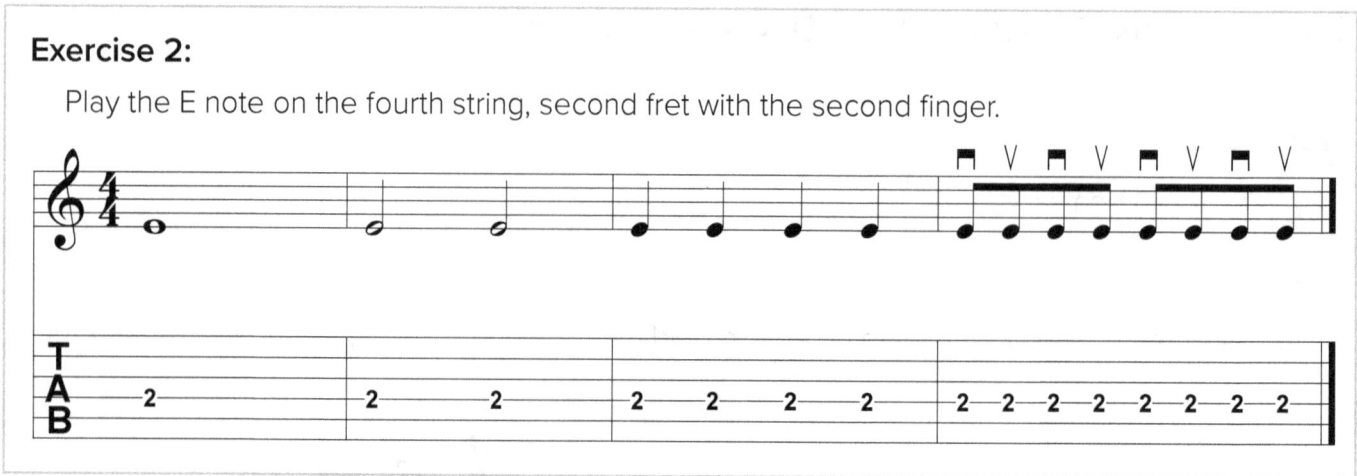

Exercise 3:
Play the F note on the fourth string, third fret with the third finger.

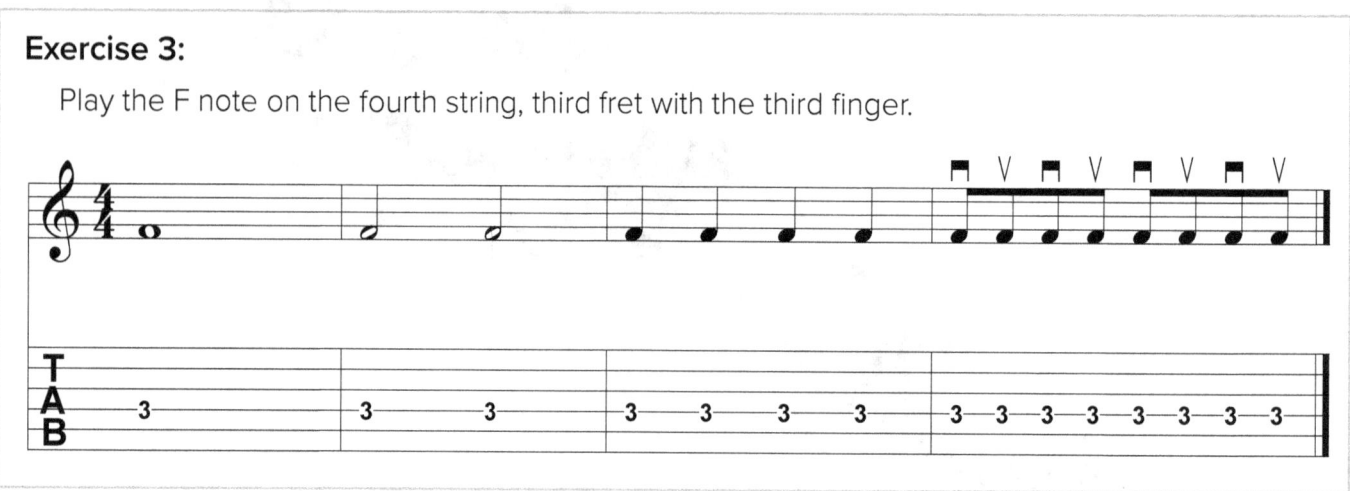

Exercise 4:
Play all three notes of the fourth string without TAB.

Review:

- Play the octave exercise on the following page (Exercise 5). Then play Exercise 17 from Lesson 7.
- From Lesson 4, review Exercise 11.

Exercise 5:

Play the octaves below.

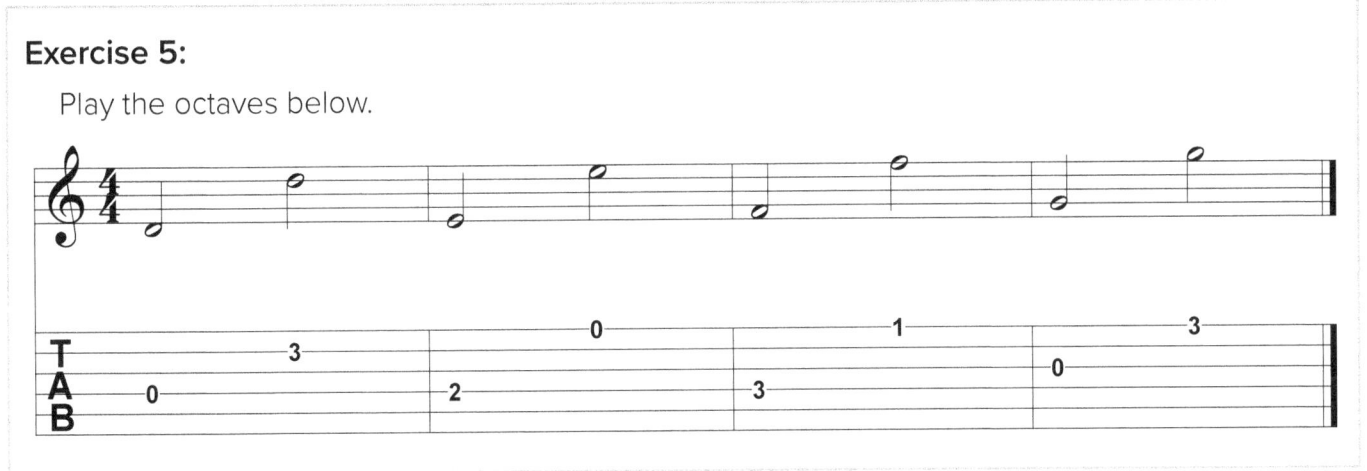

DAY 2 PRACTICE: NOTES ON THE 4ᵀᴴ STRING WITHOUT TAB

Warm-Up:

Play Exercise 11 from Lesson 6.

New:

For today's practice, you'll practice reading the notes on the fourth string without tablature. Then you'll be playing them along with the notes from the first three strings.

Exercise 6:

Play the notes of the fourth string without TAB.

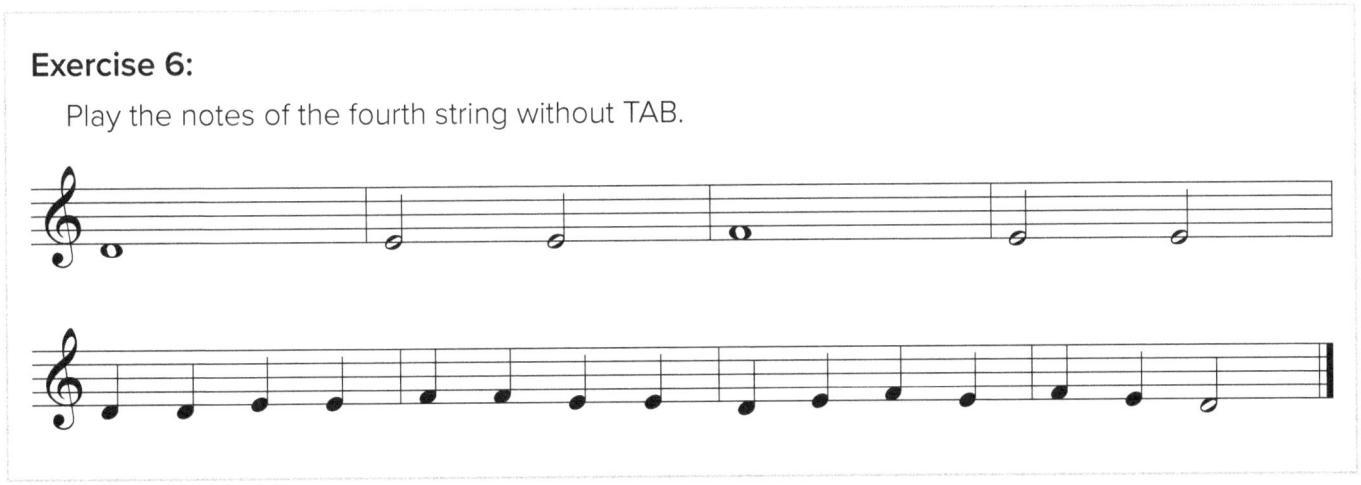

Exercise 7:

Play the notes of the fourth string along with the notes learned in Lesson 7.

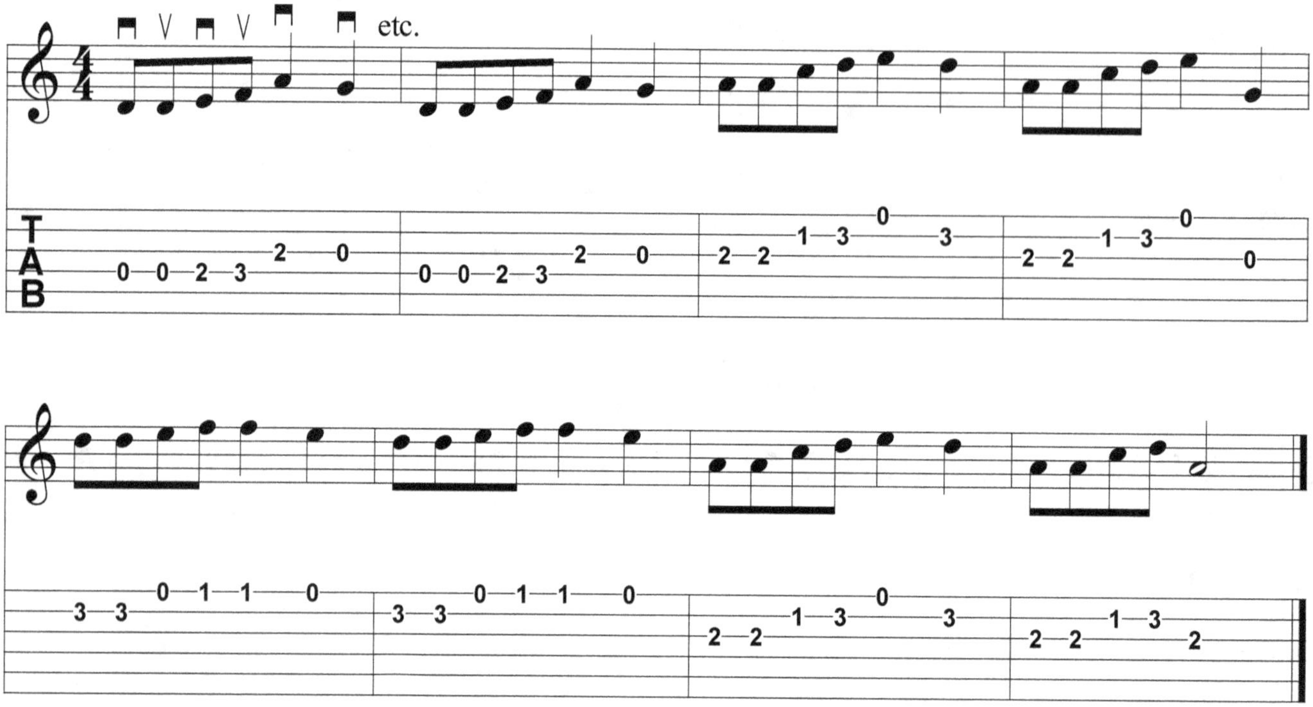

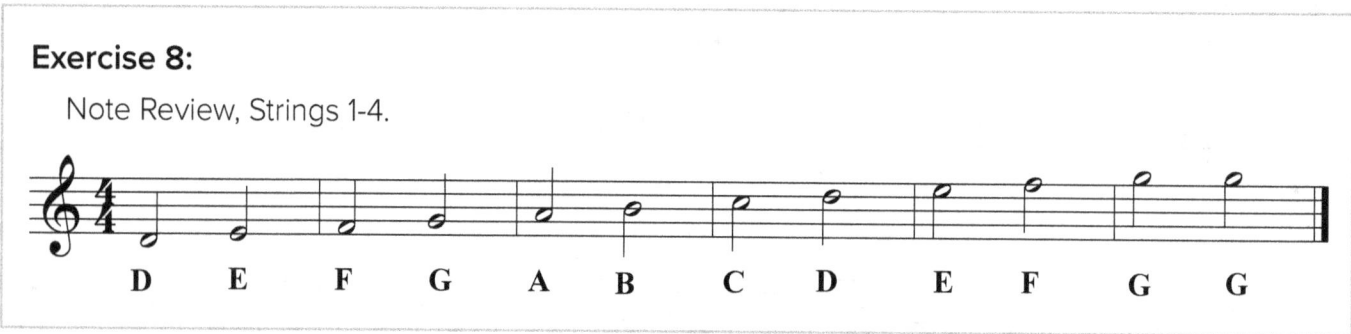

Review:

- Play the exercise below. Then play Exercises 4 and 5.
- From Lesson 4, review Exercise 12.

Exercise 8:

Note Review, Strings 1-4.

D E F G A B C D E F G G

DAY 3 PRACTICE: NOTES ON THE FIFTH STRING

Warm-Up:

Play Exercise 12 from Lesson 6.

New:

For today's practice, you'll learn how to read the notes A, B, and C on the fifth string.

Exercise 9:

Play the A note on the fifth string open. Note that the A note is two ledger lines below the staff.

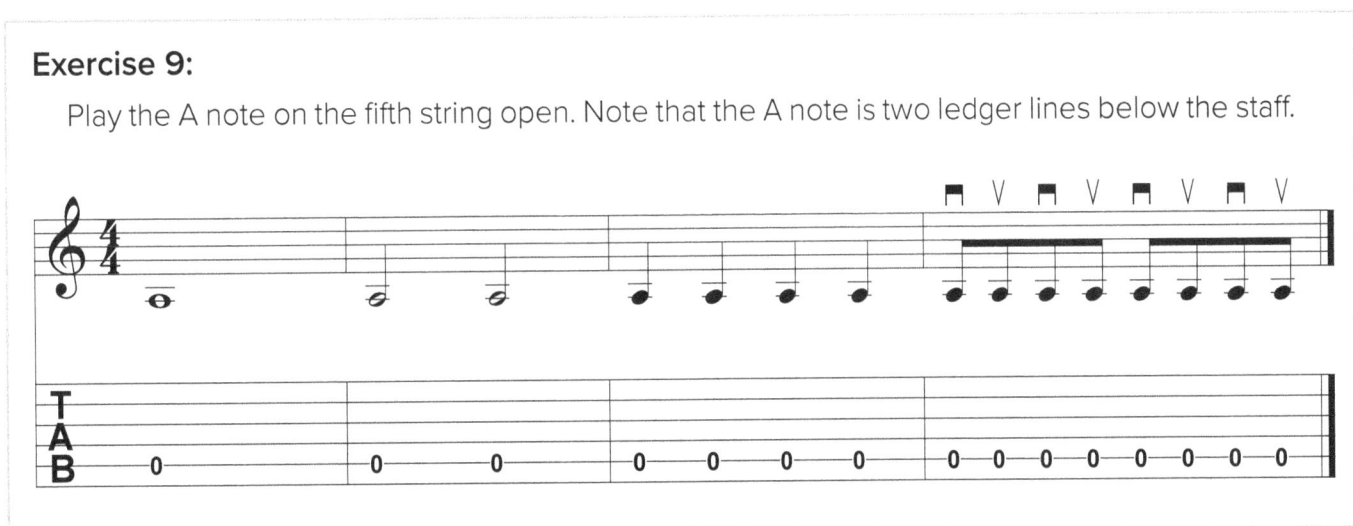

Exercise 10:

Play the B note on the fifth string, second fret with the second finger. Note that the B note is one ledger line below the staff.

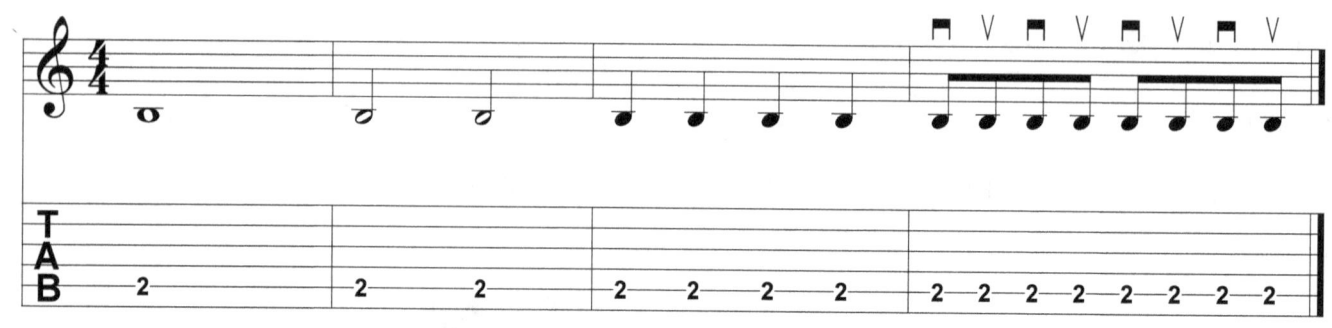

Exercise 11:

Play the C note on the fifth string, third fret with the third finger. Note that the C note is one ledger line below the staff, but this time it goes through the line.

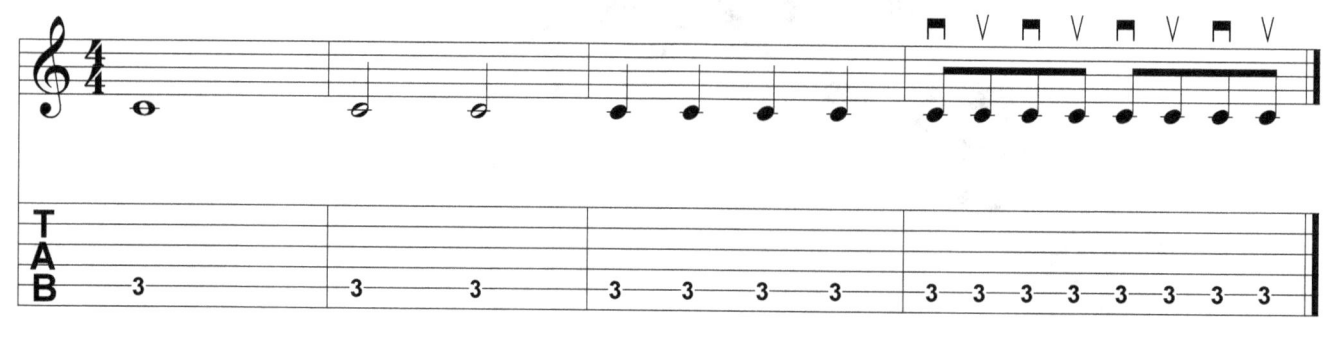

Exercise 12:

Practice the notes on the fifth string without TAB.

Review:

- Play the octave exercise below. Then play Exercises 4, 5, 6, 7, and 8.
- From Lesson 4, review Exercise 13.

Exercise 13:

Practice the octaves.

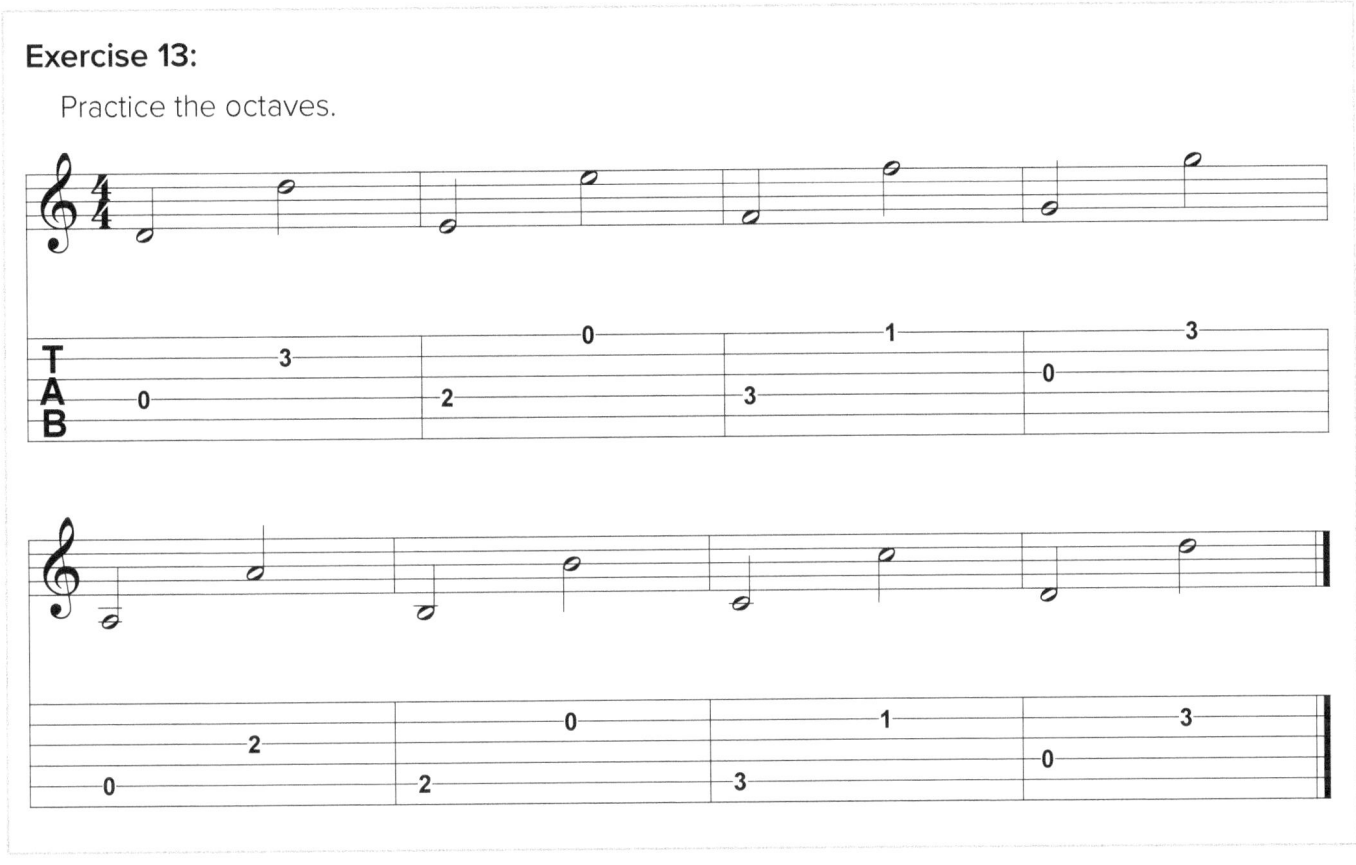

DAY 4 PRACTICE: NOTES ON STRINGS 1-5

Warm-Up:

Play Exercise 11 from Lesson 6.

New:

For today's practice, you'll practice reading the notes on the fifth string without tablature. Then you'll be playing them along with the notes from the first four strings.

Exercise 14:

Practice reading the notes on the fifth string.

Exercise 15:

Practice reading the notes on strings 1-5.

La Lune Tune

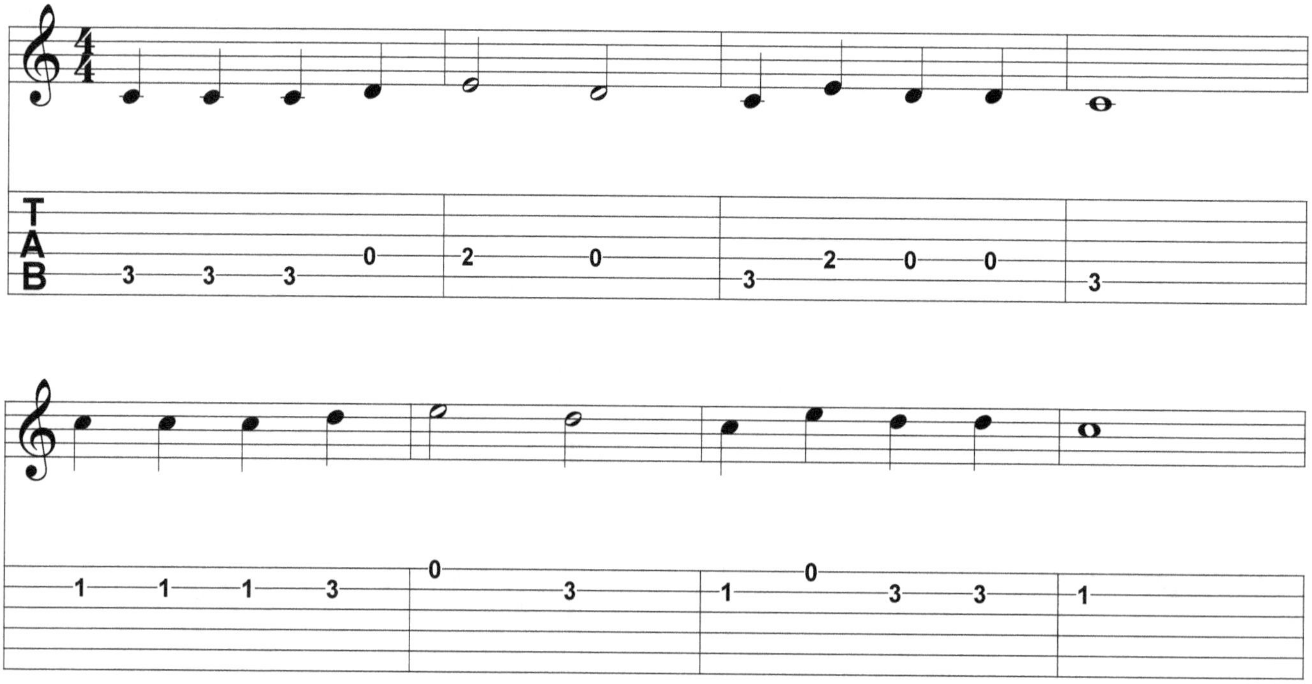

(Continued on next page.)

Review:

Play Exercises 4, 5, 6, 7, 8, and 12.

DAY 5 PRACTICE: NOTES ON THE SIXTH STRING

Warm-Up:

Play Exercise 12 from Lesson 6.

New:

For today's practice, you'll learn how to read the notes E, F, and G on the sixth string.

Exercise 16:

Play the E note on the open sixth string. Note that the low E note is under three ledger lines below the staff.

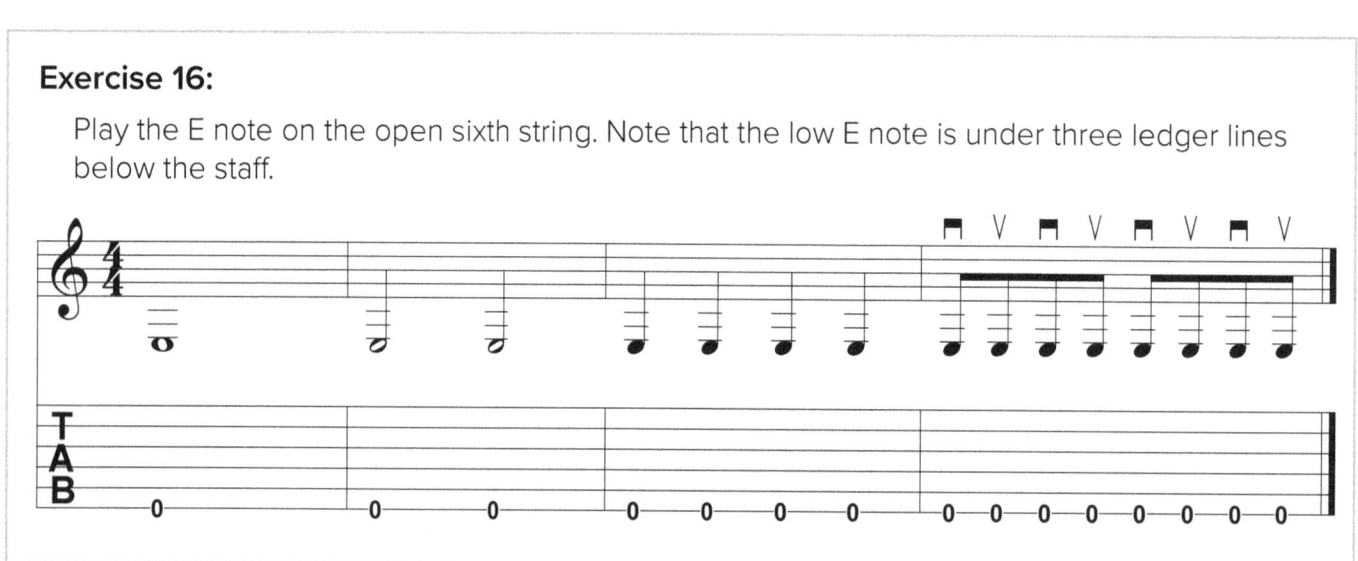

Exercise 17:

Play the F note on the sixth string, first fret with the first finger. Note that the low F note has three ledger lines, but is through the lowest line.

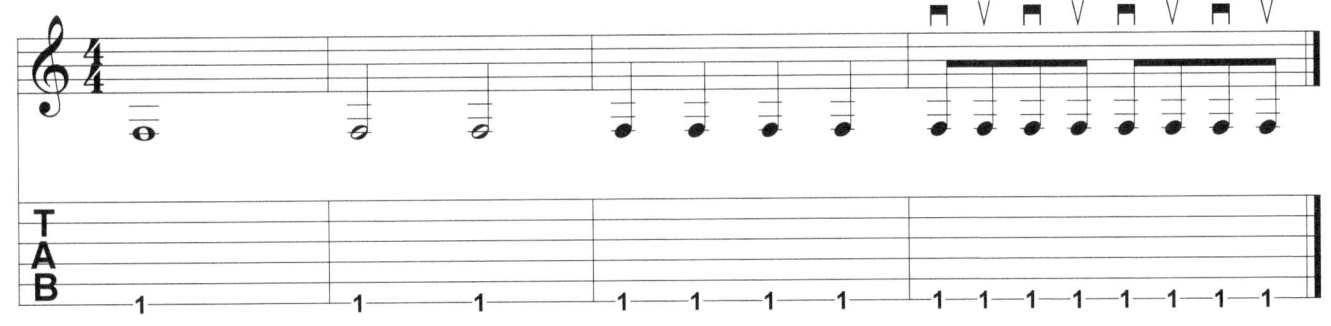

Exercise 18:

Play the G note on the sixth string, third fret with the third finger. Note that the low G note is under two ledger lines.

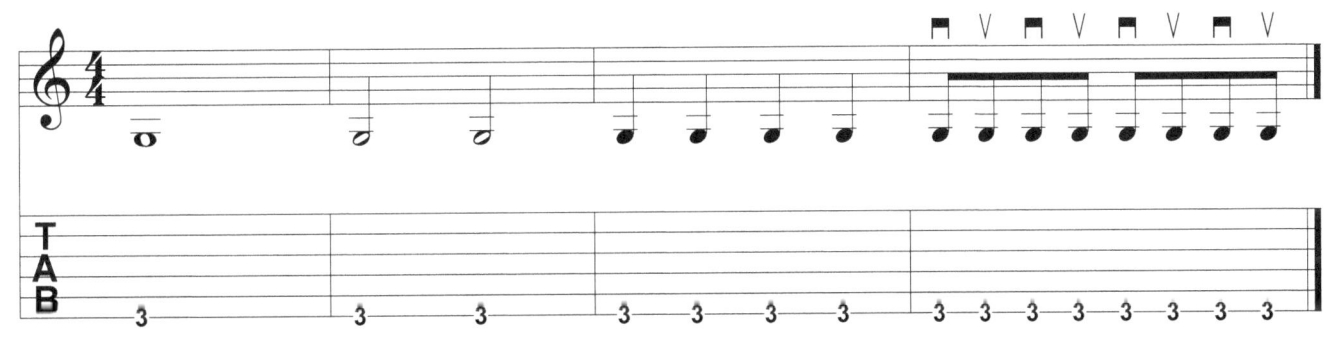

Exercise 19:

Practice the notes on the sixth string without TAB.

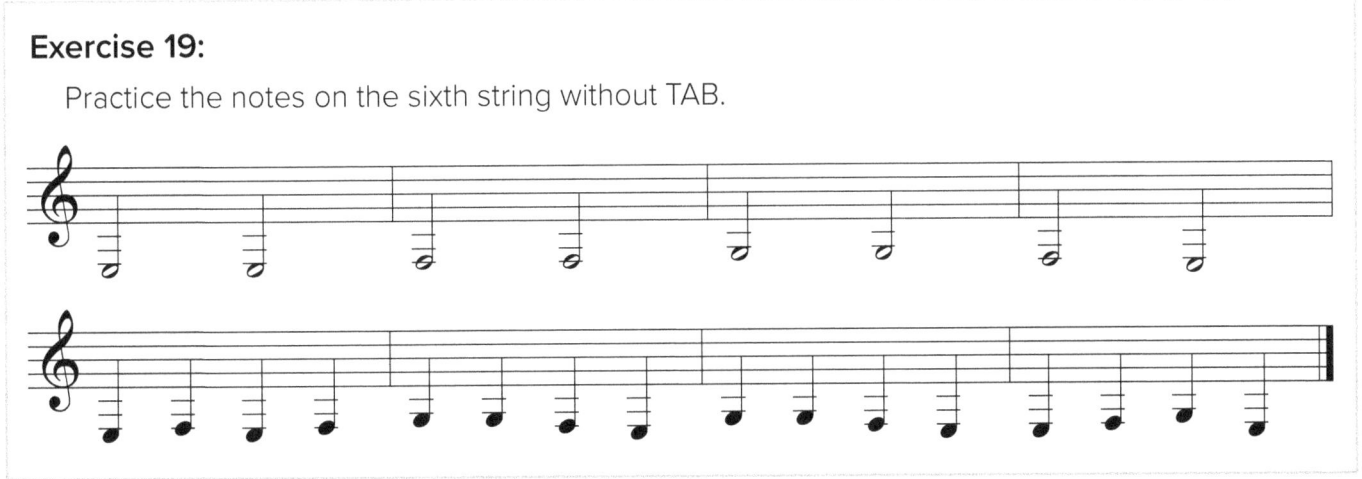

Review:

Play Exercises 4, 5, 6, 7, 8, 12, and 15.

DAY 6 PRACTICE: NOTES ON STRINGS 1-6

Warm-Up:

Play Exercise 11 from Lesson 6.

New:

For today's practice, you'll be reviewing the notes on all six strings.

Exercise 20:

Practice the notes below, saying the notes names as you play them.

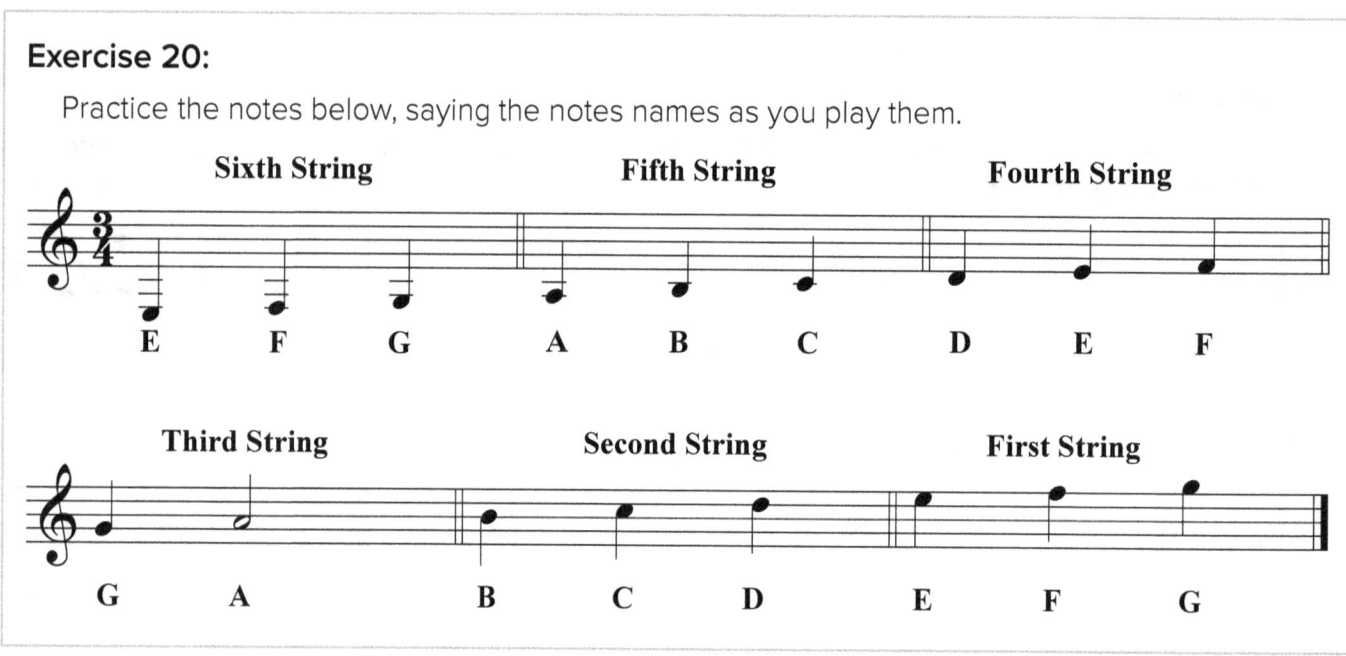

Exercise 21:

Practice the melody below.

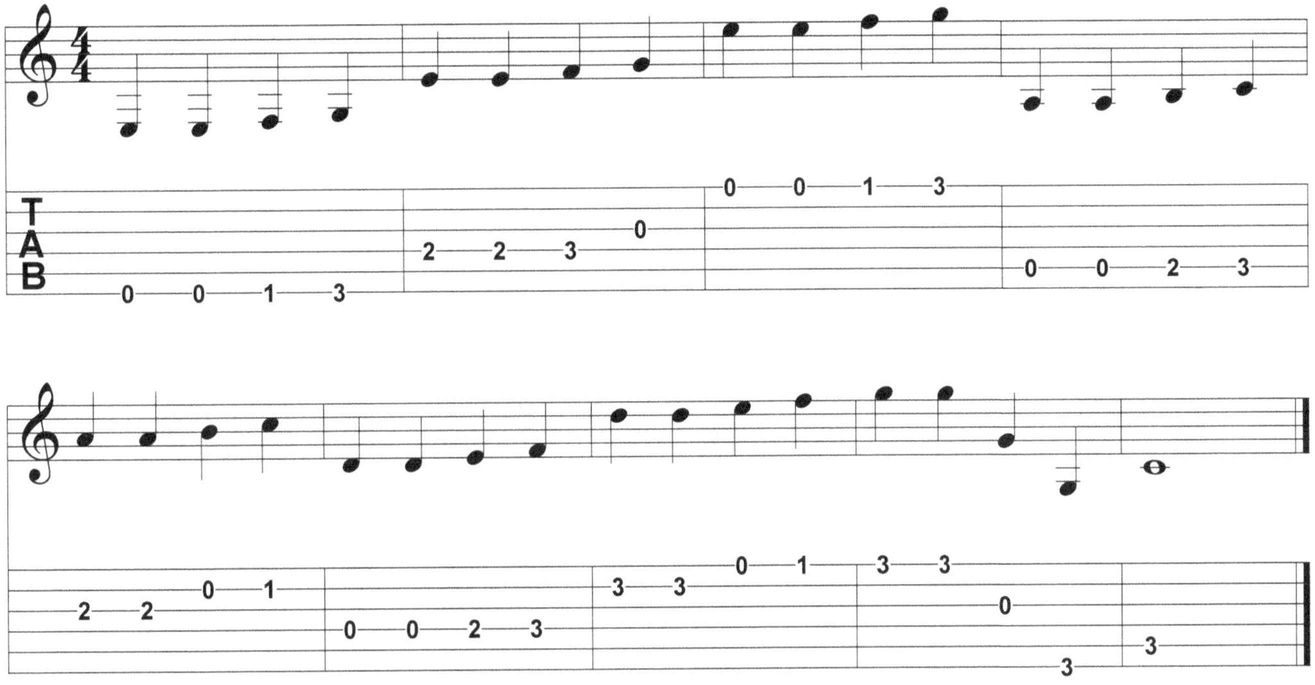

Exercise 22:

Practice the melody below, this time without the aid of TAB.

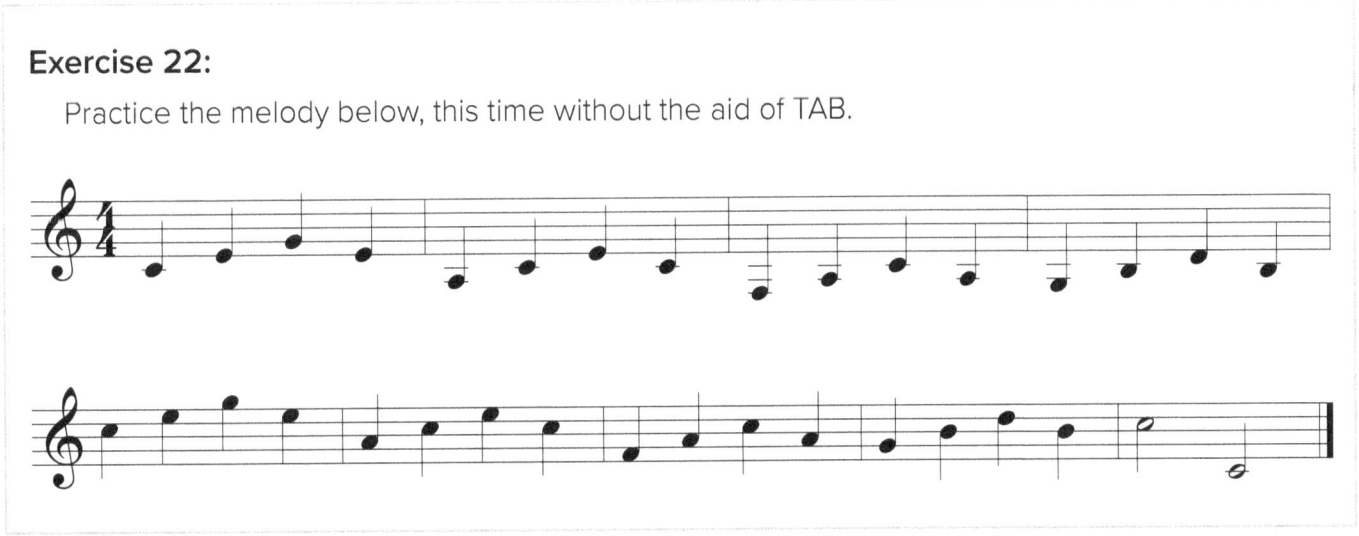

Review:

Play Exercises 4, 5, 6, 7, 8, 12, 15, and 19.

LESSON 9

READING ACCIDENTALS

The smallest distance between two notes is called a half step. To play a half step on the guitar, start anywhere on the neck and then play a note one fret higher or lower. Playing a half step higher is called sharp (#). Playing a half step lower is called flat (♭). To return to the regular note, a natural sign (♮) is used, canceling out a previous sharp or flat. These three symbols (sharp, flat, and natural) are referred to as accidentals.

Accidentals

♯ = Sharp
♭ = Flat
♮ = Natural

DAY 1 PRACTICE: READING SHARPS

Warm-Up:

Play Exercise 11 or 12 from Lesson 6.

New:

For today's practice, you'll be reading sharps. The most common sharp is F# (pronounced "F sharp"). Since there are three different F notes in open position, this means that there are three F sharps as well. One important thing to remember: once a note is sharp in a measure, all the notes of the same type are sharp until the end of the measure. So if the first F is sharp, all the remaining F's in that same measure are sharp, regardless of octave.

Exercise 1:

Practice the high F#, which is played on the first string, second fret with the second finger. Remember once a note is sharp, it stays sharp for the whole measure.

94

Exercise 2:

Practice the middle F#, which is played on the fourth string, fourth fret with the fourth finger. The fourth finger is usually the weakest finger, so it may take time before you can play this one comfortably.

Exercise 3:

Practice the low F#, which is played on the sixth string, second fret with the second finger.

Exercise 4:

Use the note F# in a melody.

Review:

Play Exercises 12, 15, 19, and 22 from Lesson 8 and Exercise 11 from Lesson 4.

DAY 2 PRACTICE: READING SHARPS, PART 2

Warm-Up:

Play Exercise 12 from Lesson 6.

New:

Now that you understand how sharps work, we are going to practice a variety of sharps in the next couple of exercises. The TAB has been included to help you figure it out, but don't rely on it exclusively.

Exercise 5:

Practice the melody below.

Exercise 6:

Try this out without the use of TAB.

Review:

Play Exercises 12, 15, 19, and 22 from Lesson 8; and from Lesson 4, play Exercise 12.

DAY 3 PRACTICE: READING FLATS

Warm-Up:

Play Exercise 11 from Lesson 6.

New:

For today's practice, you'll be reading flats. As I mentioned earlier, a flat is a half step lower than the natural note. The most common flat is B-flat, which you'll be practicing for today's practice session.

Exercise 7:

The B♭ is played on the third string at the third fret with the third finger.

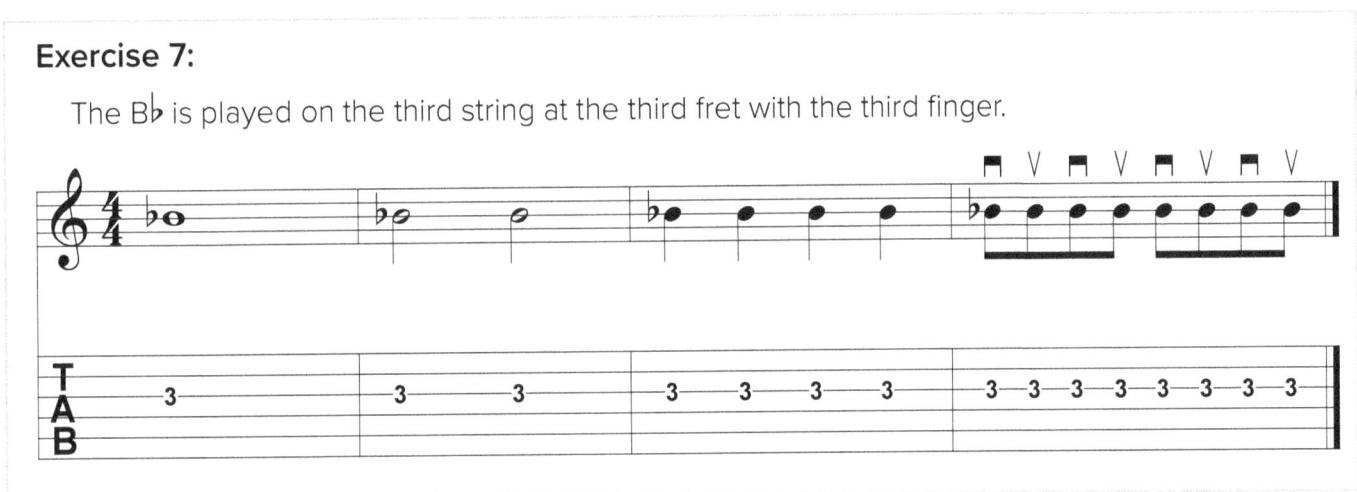

Exercise 8:

The low B♭ is played on the fifth string at the first fret with the first finger.

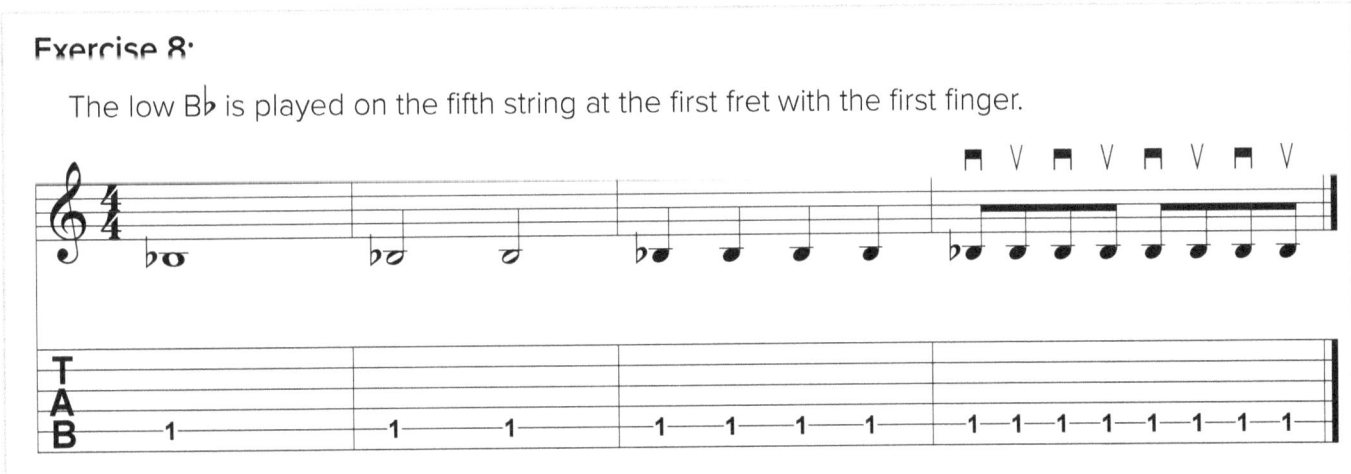

(Continue to Exercise 9 on the next page.)

Exercise 9:

Use the note B♭ in a melody.

Review:

Play Exercises 4, 5, and 6; then play Exercises 21 and 22 from Lesson 8.

DAY 4 PRACTICE: READING FLATS, PART 2

Warm-Up:

Play Exercise 12 from Lesson 6.

New:

Now that you understand how flats work, we are going to practice a variety of them in the next couple of exercises. The TAB has been included to help you figure it out, but don't rely on it exclusively.

Exercise 10:

Practice the melody below.

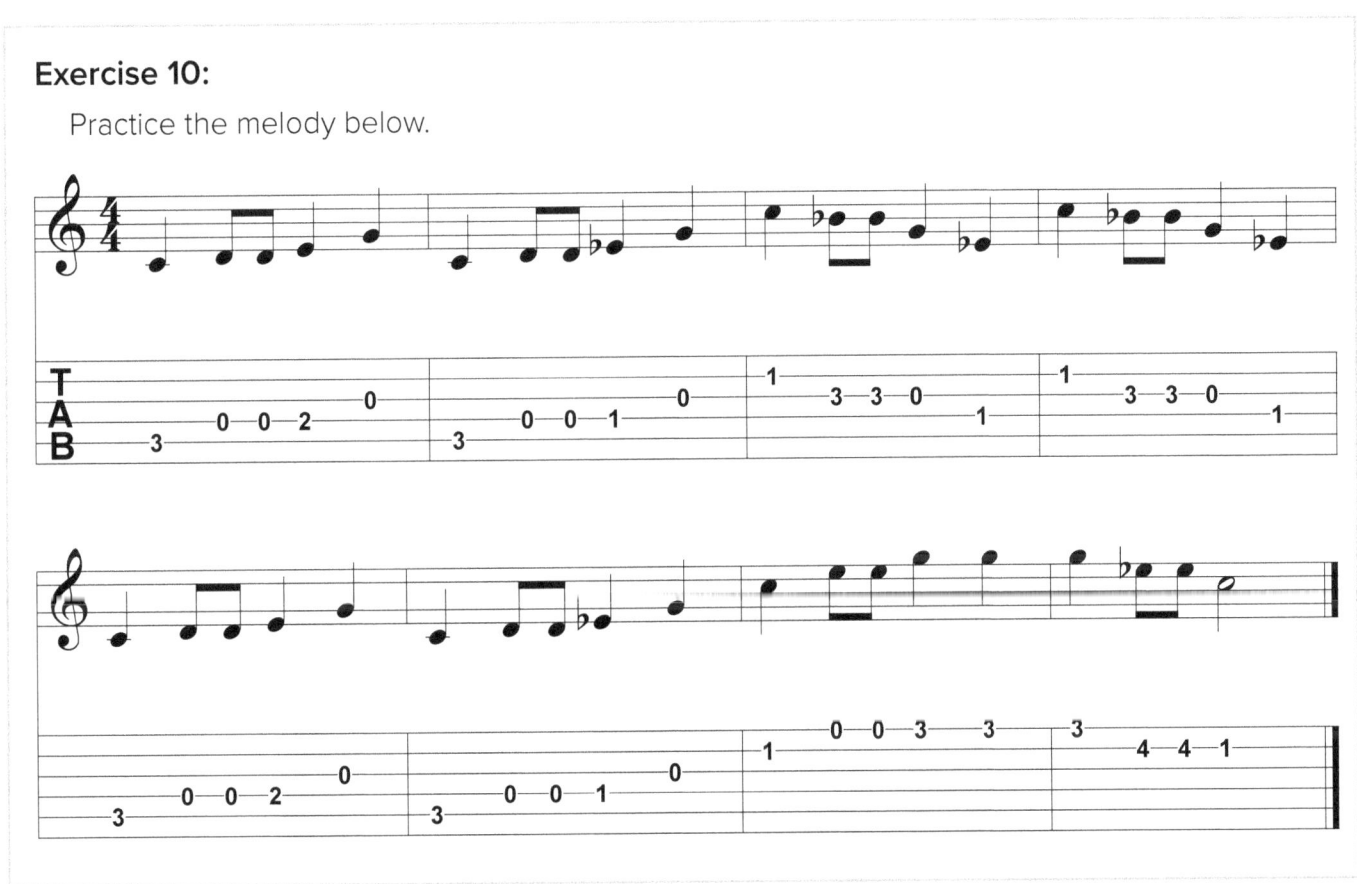

Review:

Play Exercises 4, 5, 6, and 9; then from Lesson 8, play Exercises 20, 21, and 22.

DAY 5 PRACTICE: READING NATURALS

Warm-Up:

Play Exercise 11 from Lesson 6.

New:

The natural sign (♮) cancels out a sharp or flat, returning the note to its original pitch.

Exercise 11:
Practice reading naturals.

Exercise 12:
Practice reading naturals in this melody.

Review:

Play Exercises 4, 5, 6, 9, and 10.

DAY 6 PRACTICE: KEY SIGNATURES

A lot of the time, accidentals are placed at the beginning of a song just before the time signature rather than popping up in the middle of a measure. When this is done, it is called a **key signature**.

For example, if a sharp sign is placed on the "F" line that tells you that all the F's in the song are sharp, regardless of octave. The same idea is applied to flats as well.

Key signatures tell us more than what is sharp or flat, but that gets complicated quickly. For now, just know that when you see a sharp, flat, or many sharps or flats at the beginning of a song, that means those notes have been changed so the that the key sounds the way it is supposed to.

Example Key Signatures:

 This means that all the F's are sharp.

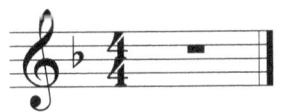 This means that all the B's are flat.

 This means that all the F's, C's, G's, and D's are sharp.

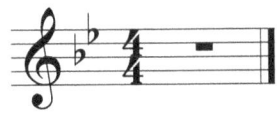 This means that all the B's and E's are flat.

Warm-Up:

Play Exercise 12 from Lesson 6.

New:

Practice key signatures with Exercises 13 & 14.

Exercise 13:

Practice reading with this key signature.

Exercise 14:

Practice reading with this key signature.

Review:

- Play Exercises 4, 5, 6, 9, 10, and 12.
- From Lesson 4, review Exercises 6, 7, and 8.
- From Lesson 5, review 4, 5, 6, and 7.

LESSON 10

FINGERSTYLE PLAYING

Fingerstyle guitar is the original way of playing the instrument. Instead of using a pick, you use your thumb and first three fingers to pluck the strings. There are many approaches to this style, ranging from classical music approaches to self-accompanied country. Here we will cover the basics of fingerstyle.

The general rule of this approach is that the thumb plays notes on the three bass strings, or strings D, A, and low E. The index finger plucks the third string (G); the middle finger plays the second string (B); and the ring finger plays the first string (E).

Fingerstyle was popularized in Spain, so most of the terminology is in Spanish, including the symbols used in sheet music. Therefore, P=Pulgar (thumb); i=indice (index); m=medio (middle); and a=anular (ring finger). The pinky is not typically used in this style of playing.

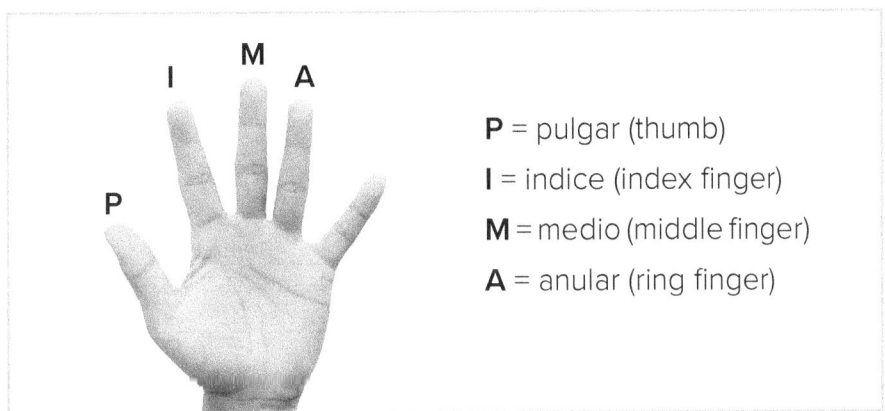

BASIC FINGERSTYLE TECHNIQUE

Step 1: Before you try it, place all four fingers into position, meaning that each finger will be placed on their assigned string. This is something you'll always want to do before fingerpicking.

Step 2: Once you have all your fingers (including the thumb) in place, start by plucking the sixth string with the thumb, but continue to keep your other fingers on the strings.

Step 3: Next, pluck the third string with the index finger. When you do this, only move from the middle knuckle of your hand, pulling inward toward your palm, so as to minimize movement in your picking hand.

Step 4: Next, pluck the second string in the same manner, pulling your finger into your palm.

Step 5: Finally, do the same with the ring finger on the first string.

Note: Your fingers should be curved, and your wrist should NOT be lying flat. It too should be curved. Again, always prepare your fingers on the strings before playing. (See photo on the next page.)

Keep your fingers relaxed. The thumb rests on top of the lowest (6th) string. The rest of the fingers curl naturally under, ready to pluck their assigned string. The wrist also curves naturally to make it easy for the fingers to remain relaxed and in place.

Try it: Hold down the G Chord as you play this example

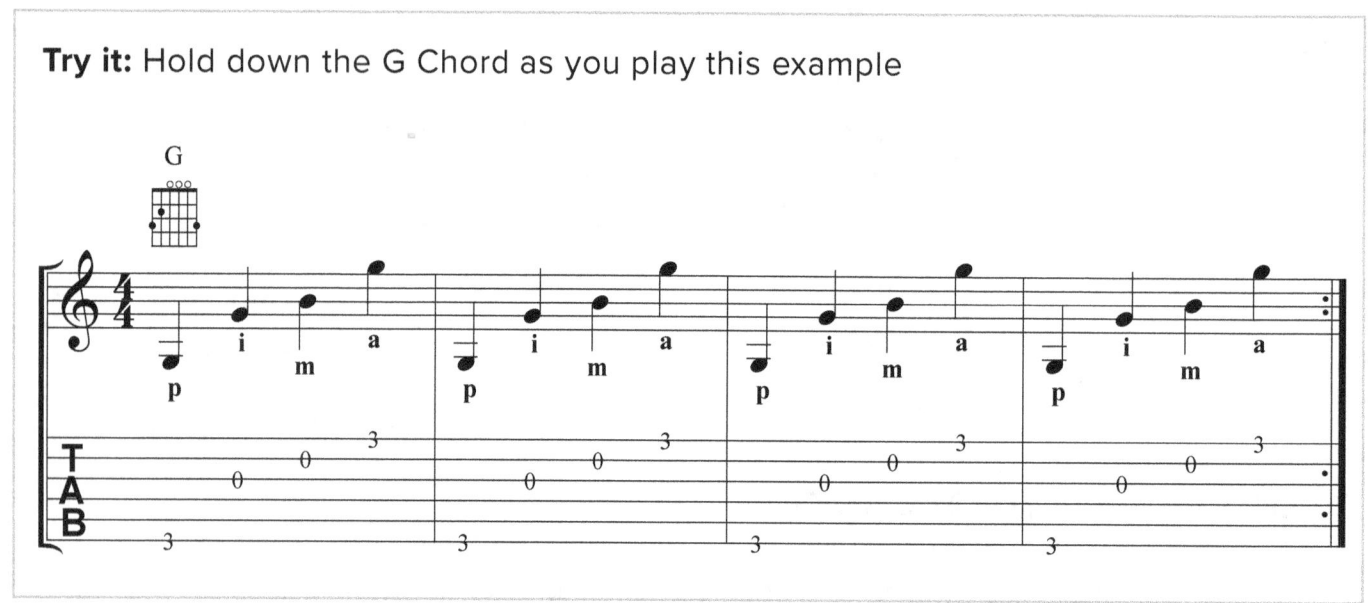

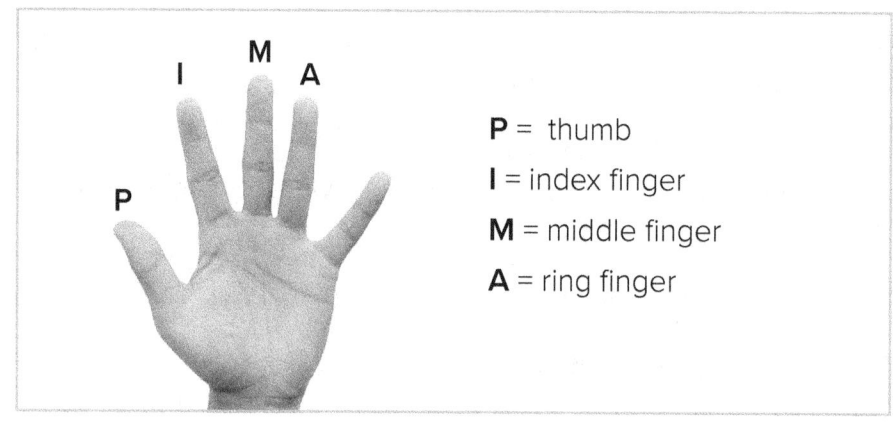

P = thumb
I = index finger
M = middle finger
A = ring finger

DAY 1 PRACTICE: PIMA WITH E AND G MAJOR

Warm-Up:

Play Exercise 12 from Lesson 6.

New:

For today's practice, you'll work on practicing basic fingerpicking technique using the G and Em chords.

Exercise 1:

Practice the PIMA finger pattern using the E minor chord.

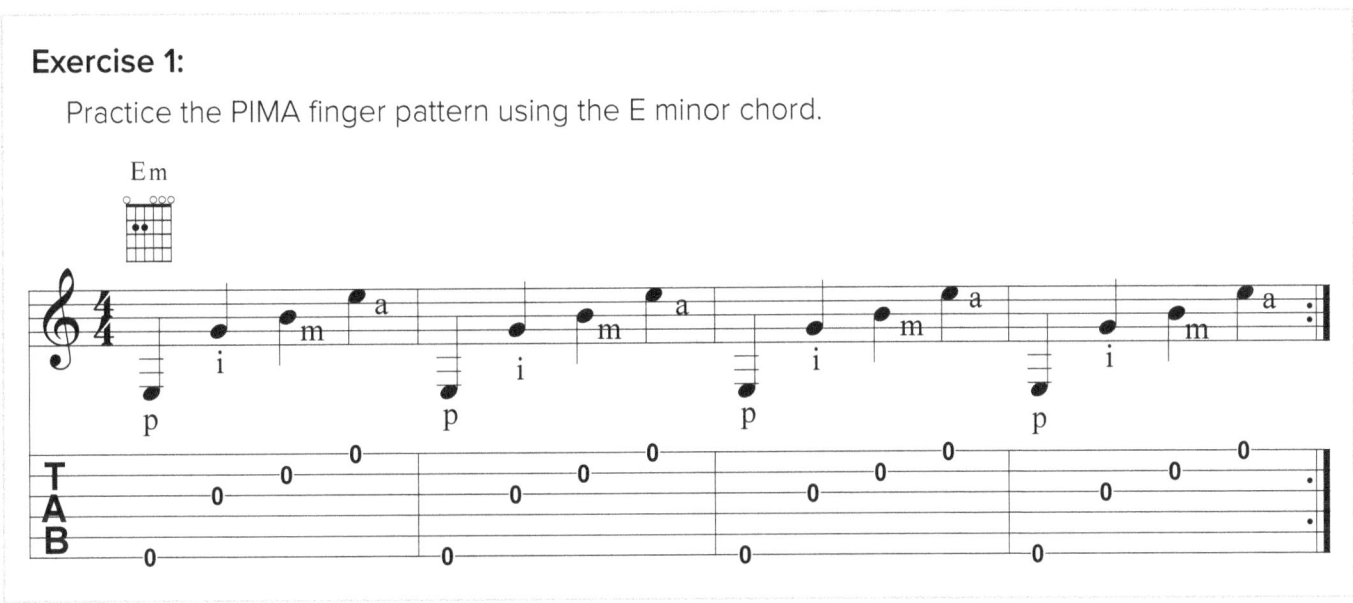

Exercise 2:

Practice the PIMA finger pattern using the G major and E minor chords.

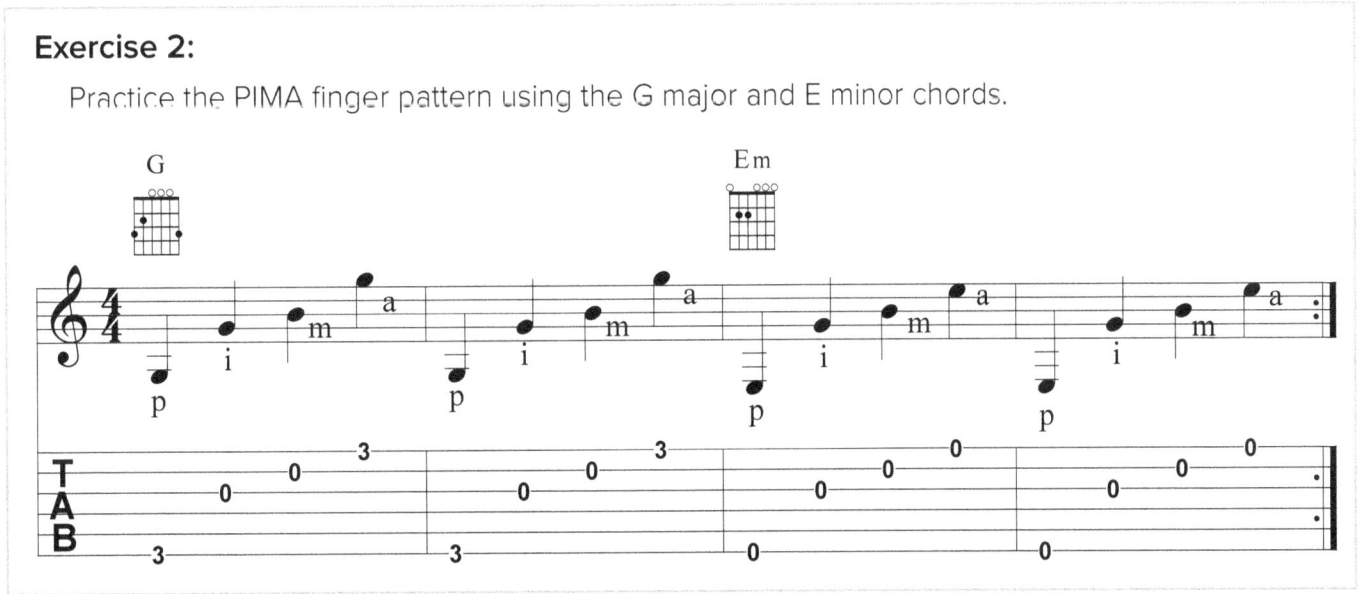

Review:

Play Exercises 12, 13, and 14 from Lesson 9.

DAY 2 PRACTICE: PIMA WITH C MAJOR AND A MINOR

Warm-Up:

Play Exercise 12 from Lesson 6.

New:

For today's practice, you'll work on practicing basic fingerpicking technique using the C and Am chords. Therefore, your thumb will now play the fifth string.

Exercise 3:

Practice the PIMA finger pattern using the C major chord.

Exercise 4:

Practice the PIMA finger pattern using the A minor chord.

Exercise 5:

Practice the PIMA finger pattern using the C, G, Am, and Em chords.

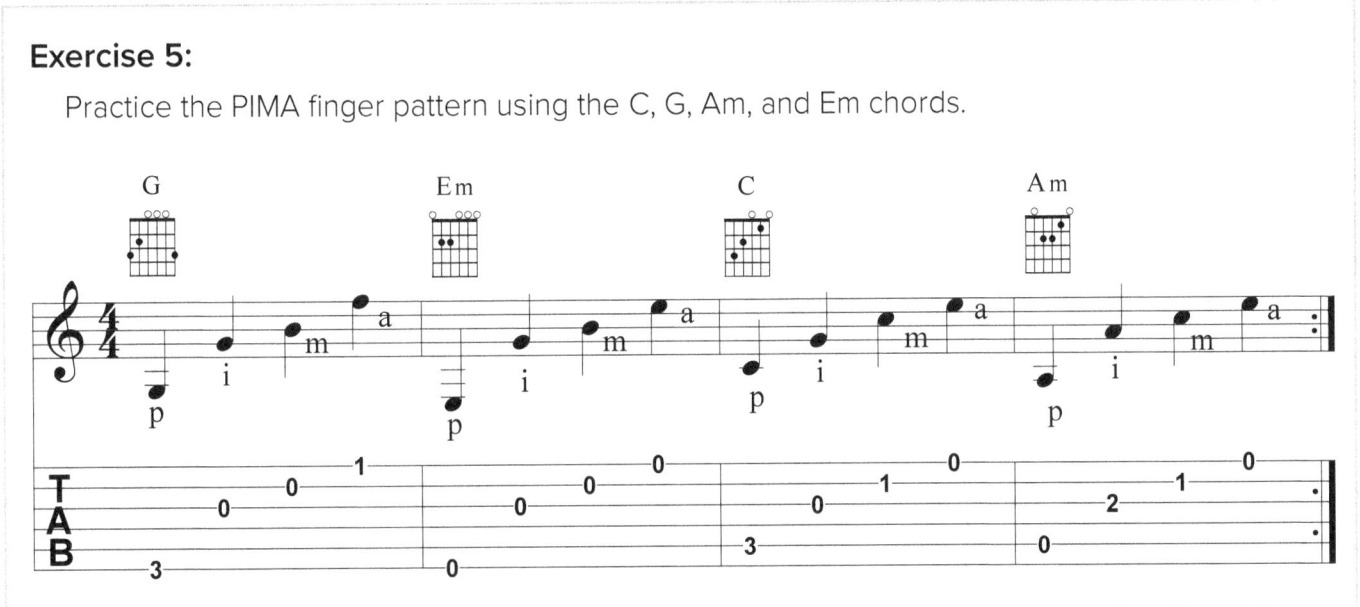

Review:

Play Exercises 1 and 2.

DAY 3 PRACTICE: PIMA WITH D MAJOR AND F MAJOR

Warm-Up:

Play Exercise 12 from Lesson 6.

New:

For today's practice, you'll practice the PIMA pattern once again, but this time your thumb will play string four.

Exercise 6:

Practice the PIMA finger pattern using the D major chord.

Exercise 7:

Practice the PIMA finger pattern using the F major chord. (Since this one can be challenging, an alternate version has been included below for ease of practice.)

Exercise 7: Alternate Version

Note that this version uses the Fmaj7 chord. To play it, simply hold down three of the notes of a regular F chord, but keep the first string open instead of using a barre.

Exercise 8:

A full fingerpicking chord progression.

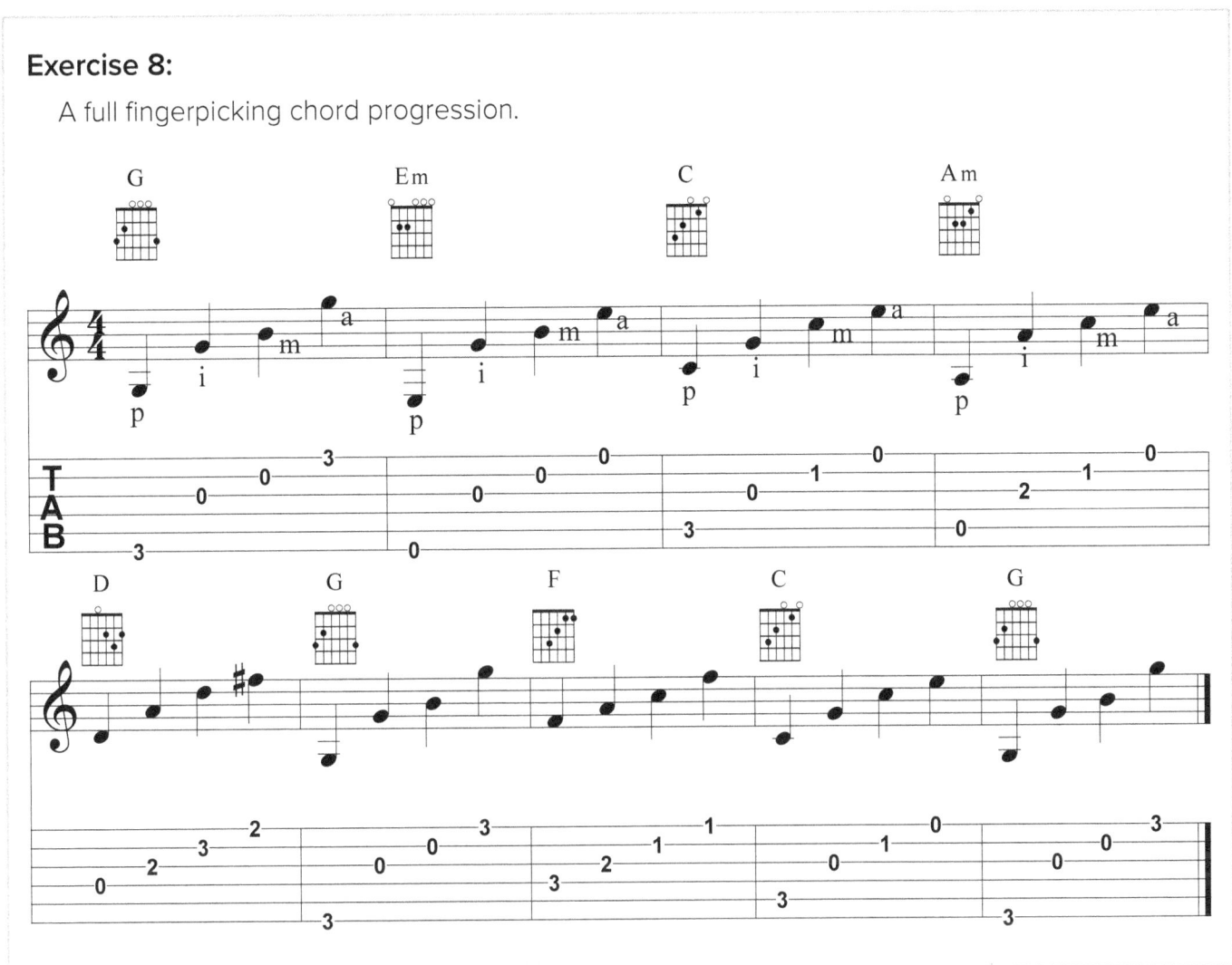

Review:

Play Exercises 2 and 5.

DAY 4 PRACTICE: PIMA-AMIP PATTERN

Warm-Up:

Play Exercise 12 from Lesson 6.

New:

For today's practice, you'll practice a new fingerpicking pattern: PIMA-AMIP.

Exercise 9:

Practice the PIMA-AMIP pattern.

Exercise 10:

Practice the PIMA-AMIP pattern with multiple chords.

Review:

Play Exercises 2, 5, and 8.

DAY 5 PRACTICE: PIMIAIMI PATTERN

Warm-Up:

Play Exercise 12 from Lesson 6.

New:

For today's practice, you'll practice the new fingerpicking pattern: PIMIAIMI.

Exercise 11:

Practice the PIMIAIMI pattern with the Em chord.

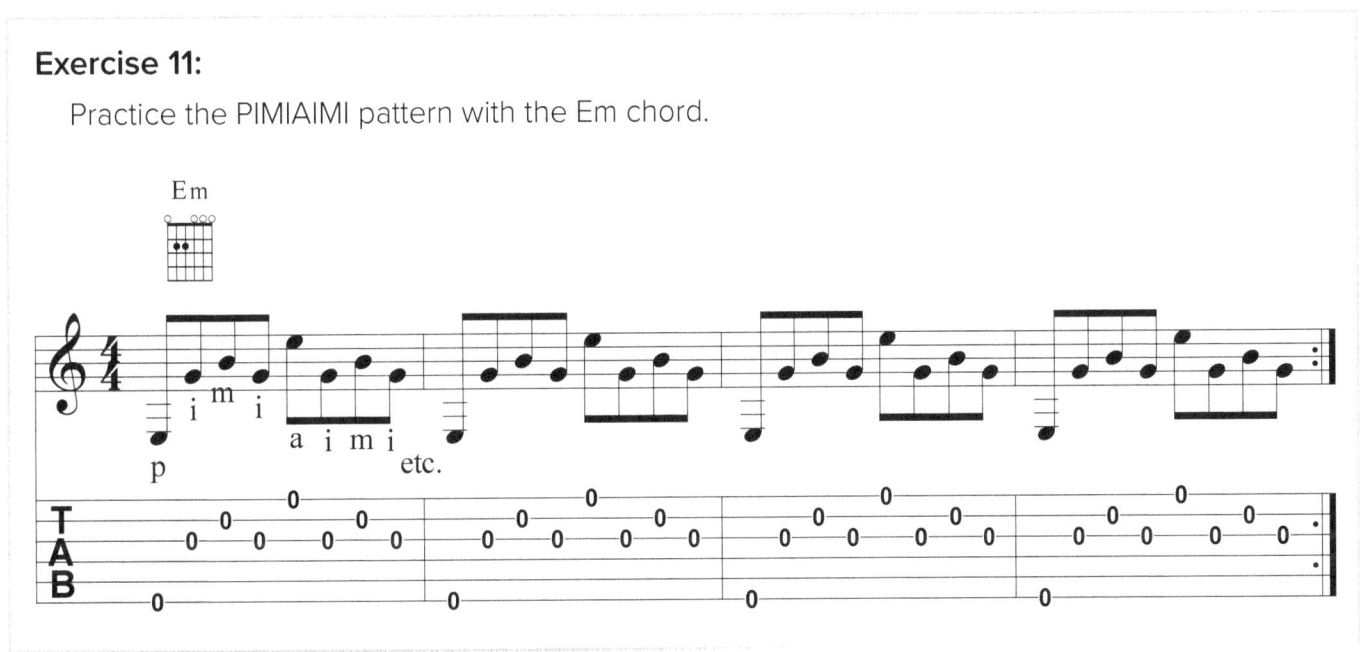

Exercise 12:

Practice the PIMIAIMI pattern with multiple chords.

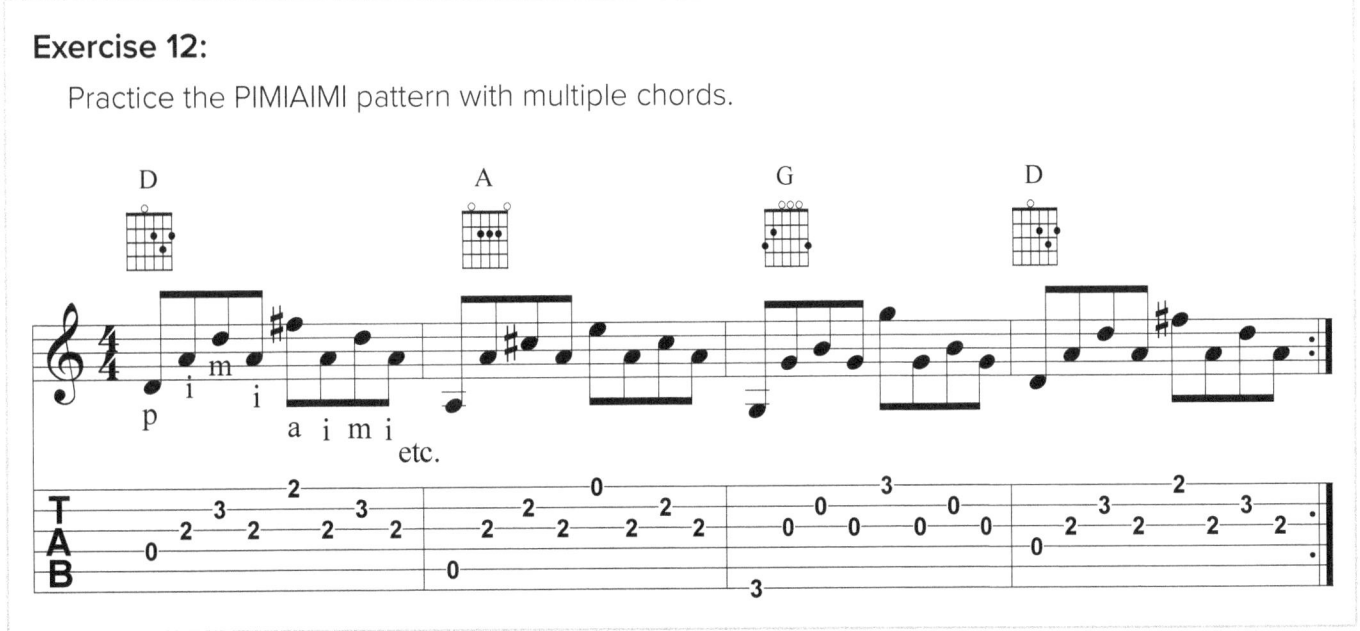

Review:

Play Exercises 2, 5, 8, and 10.

DAY 6 PRACTICE: PM-PIPMPI PATTERN

Warm-Up:

Play Exercise 12 from Lesson 6.

New:

For today's practice, you'll practice another new fingerpicking pattern. This time you'll be playing two notes at the same time on the downbeat so that your thumb and middle finger will play at the same time before moving into the rest of the pattern. So it's PM (together) followed by PIPMPI.

Exercise 13:

Practice the new pattern with the E chord.

Exercise 14:

Practice the new pattern with multiple chords.

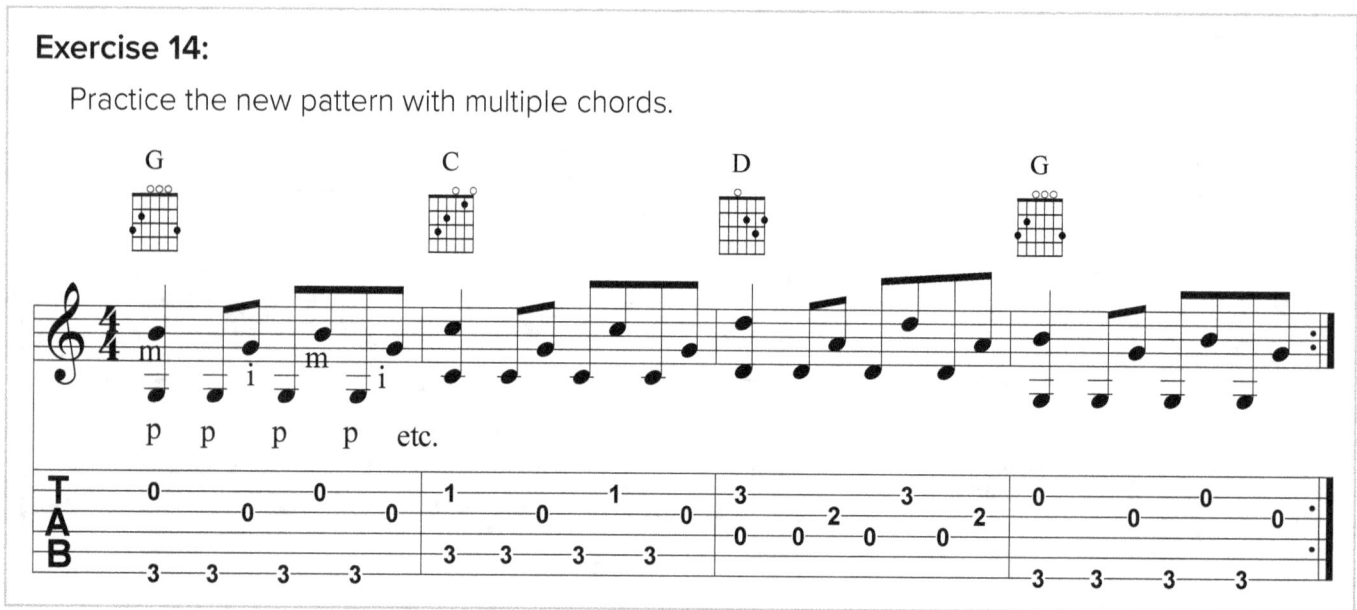

Review:

Play Exercises 2, 5, 8, 10, and 12.

SONGS FOR PRACTICE

In this section of the book, you have several songs to try out using the different skills you've acquired. The first song allows you to practice chords, the second one gives you a chance to practice reading tablature, the third is an exercise in note reading (though you can strum the chords too if you'd like), and the final song gives you a chance to put your fingerpicking skills to the test.

CHORD PRACTICE

TAB PRACTICE

For this practice with tablature, you'll be playing a common song form called the **12-bar blues**. As its name states, the basic form is 12 measures long and originated with blues music. Chords have been included in case you want to try strumming the song as a separate guitar part.

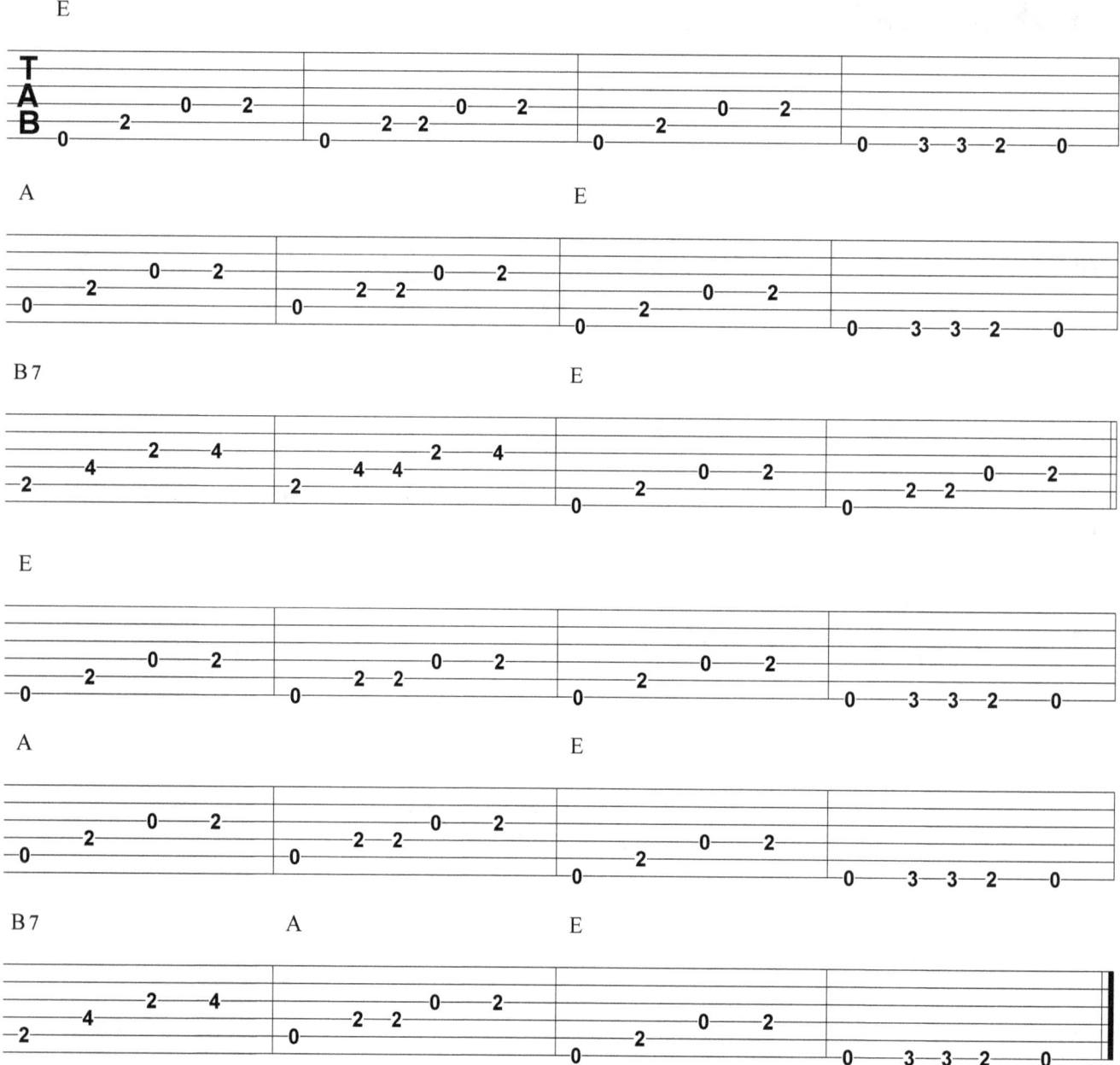

114

NOTE READING PRACTICE

Use the song below to practice note reading. This song includes two new note reading elements you'll want to be aware of:

1. **Pick-up notes**. Pick-up notes are notes found at the beginning of a song but are not part of a complete measure, as seen with the first two notes of the song below.

2. A **tie**. A tie simply connects a note to another note to lengthen how long you hold it for. You'll find an example of a tie on the "D" note at the start of line four in the song below. In this case, play the "D" and then hold it for two more beats. Chords have again been included with this song in case you want to try strumming it as a separate guitar part.

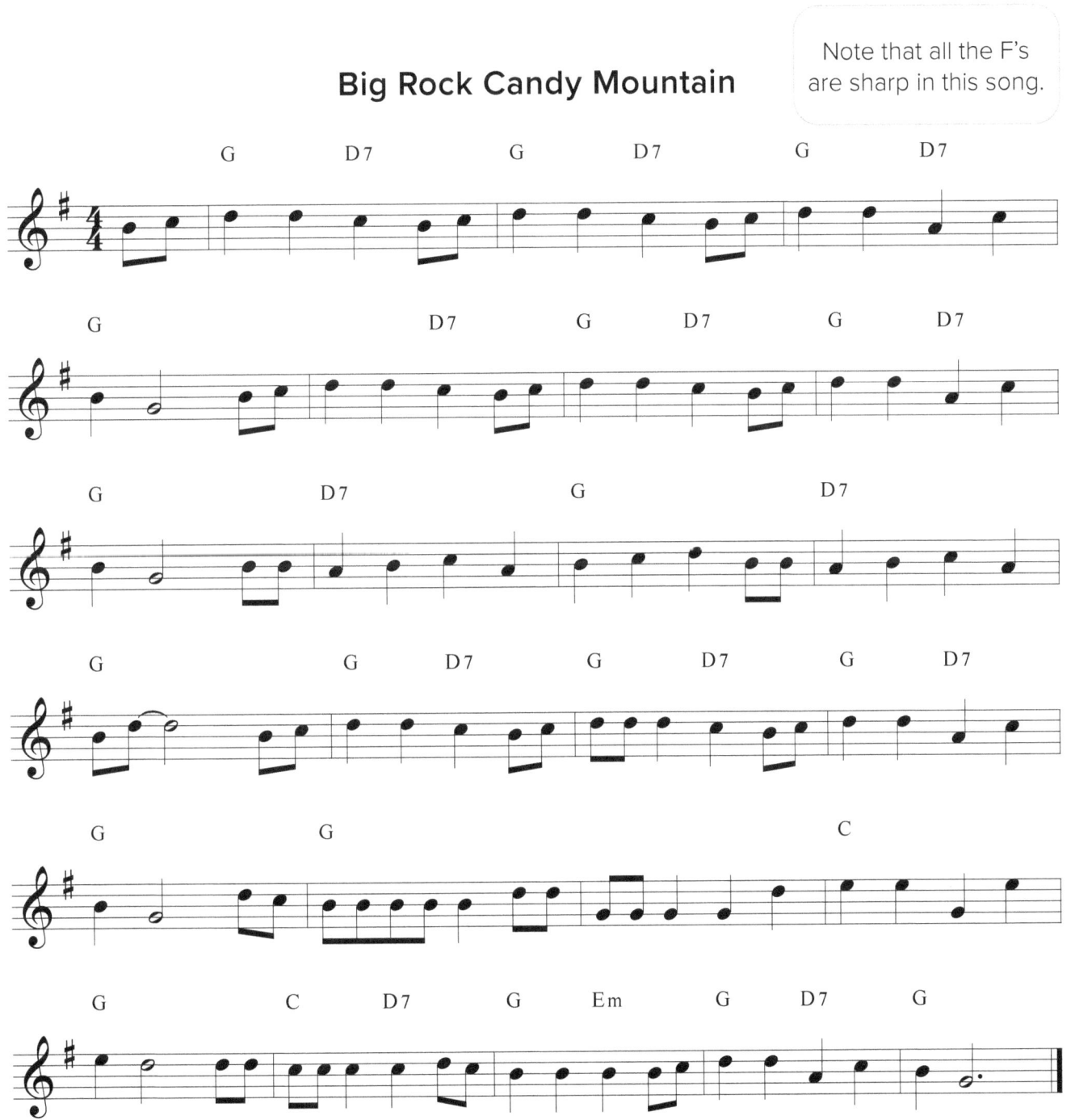

FINGERPICKING PRACTICE

Use the song below to practice fingerpicking. Note that the verses use the PIMA pattern, and the choruses use the PIMIAIMI pattern.

(Continued on the next page)

NEXT STEPS

Congratulations! You have completed *Your First Ten Guitar Lessons!* You now have the fundamental skills every acoustic guitar player should know. The question is, what come next? We recommend choosing from the following:

Option 1:
Continue learning chords and strum patterns with *Guitar Chord Master 1: Basic Chords*. The first part of the book will act as a review for you, and the second half will expand your chord vocabulary. If you've enjoyed learning and strumming chords, this is the book you'll want to get next.

Option 2:
Continue learning note reading in more depth with *The Missing Method for Guitar Note Reading Series, Book 1*. This book reviews the notes you've learned here, giving you even more practice, plus it includes more complex rhythms, and gives you an opportunity to practice note reading in all 12 keys.

Option 3:
Learn songs. Even as you develop your skills, learning songs is the best way to keep yourself motivated and learn new things as you go. To do this, we recommend exploring song books and websites like Musicnotes.com, Ultimate Guitar, or Songsterr, and of course, TheMissingMethod.com. On our site and YouTube channel, you'll find video tutorials for a lot of different songs from a variety of genres.

Option 4:
And of course, you can do any combination of the above. Many of our students work through books in the *Guitar Chord Master Series* and *Missing Method for Guitar Note Reading Series* while working on songs as well. Just be sure not to take on too much so that you become overwhelmed. Pace it out, a bit at a time with regular warm-up, new information, and review as you've done in this book, and you'll continue to see progress.

Also, don't forget to check out the chord reference and "How to Use a Capo" sections in the appendix.

Best Wishes & Happy Playing,

Christian and Amy Joy Triola

PS: Be sure to also sign up for our weekly newsletter if you haven't already. We regularly send out announcements about new releases, special discounts, and free resources that will help you become a better guitar player. Find it at https://TheMissingMethod.com/newsletter.

Further Resources

The Missing Method for Guitar specializes in creating books that make it easy for you to learn guitar. Below are a few of our offerings. If you have any questions, please feel free to email us at info@TheMissingMethod.com.

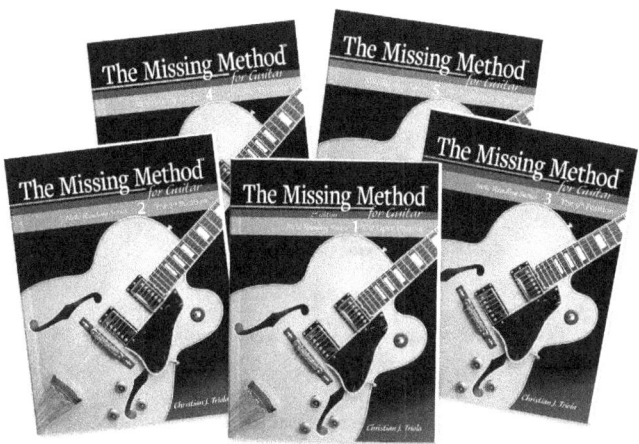

The Missing Method for Guitar Note Reading Series

Designed for note reading mastery, The Missing Method for Guitar Note Reading series works progressively from one string to the next, through every key. Book 1 starts you in open position (Frets 0-5) and each subsequent book moves further up the neck finishing with the highest notes on guitar (Frets 12-22). If you are looking to master the fretboard, this is the series for you.

Guitar Chord Master Series

Master common chord progressions and strum patterns you can use to play the songs you love. Start with basic chords in book 1 and progress to more advanced chords as you move through the series.

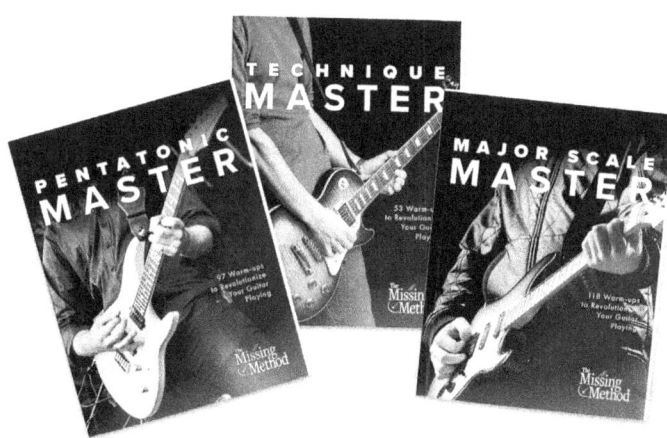

Technique Master Series

Want to know the secret to great guitar playing? It all starts with strong technique and a good set of warm-ups. With the Technique Master Series, you'll learn scales every guitar player should know as you warm-up, and you'll hone your technique in the process.

Find these and much more at TheMissingMethod.com.

APPENDIX

CHORD REFERENCE

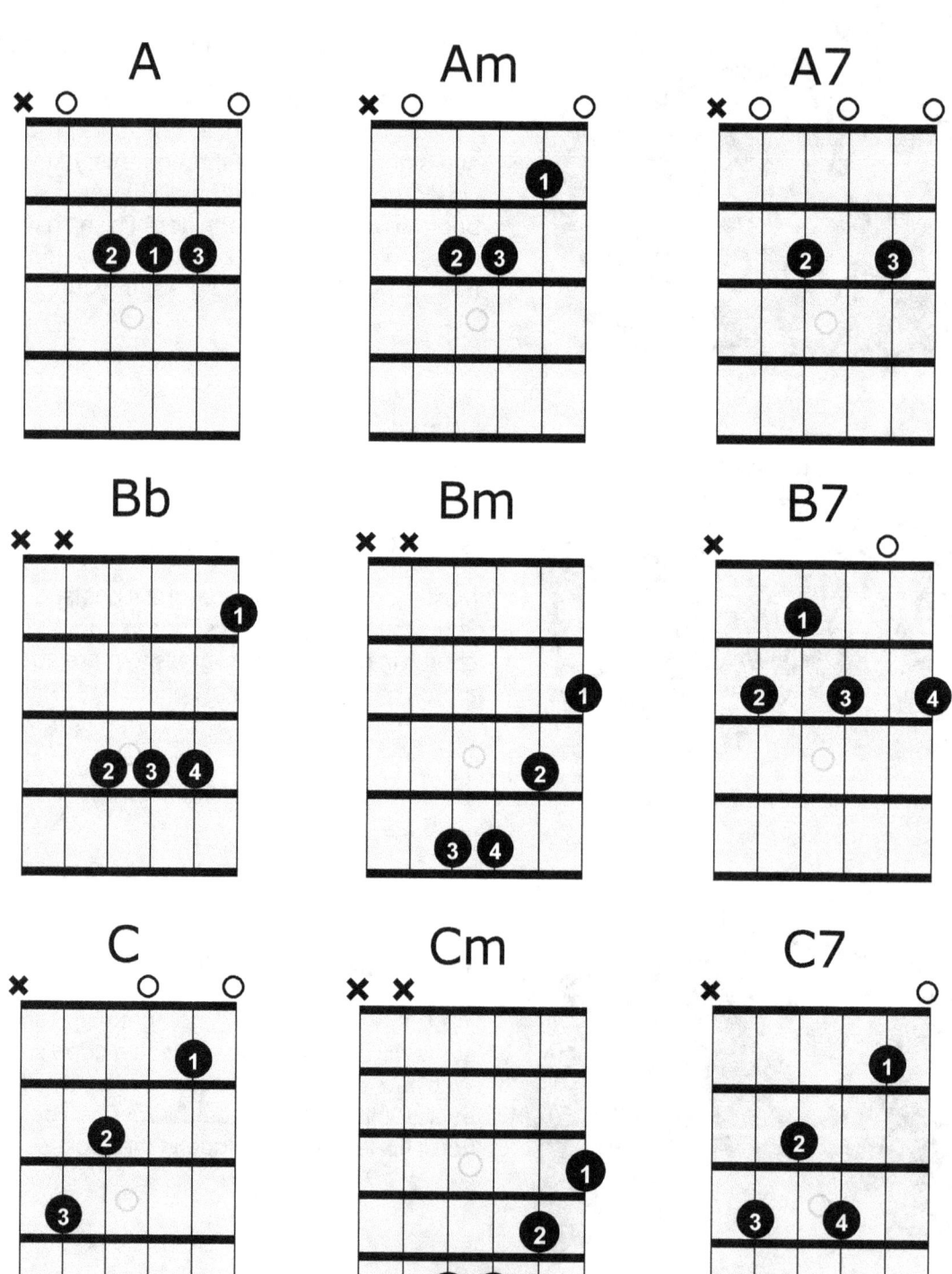

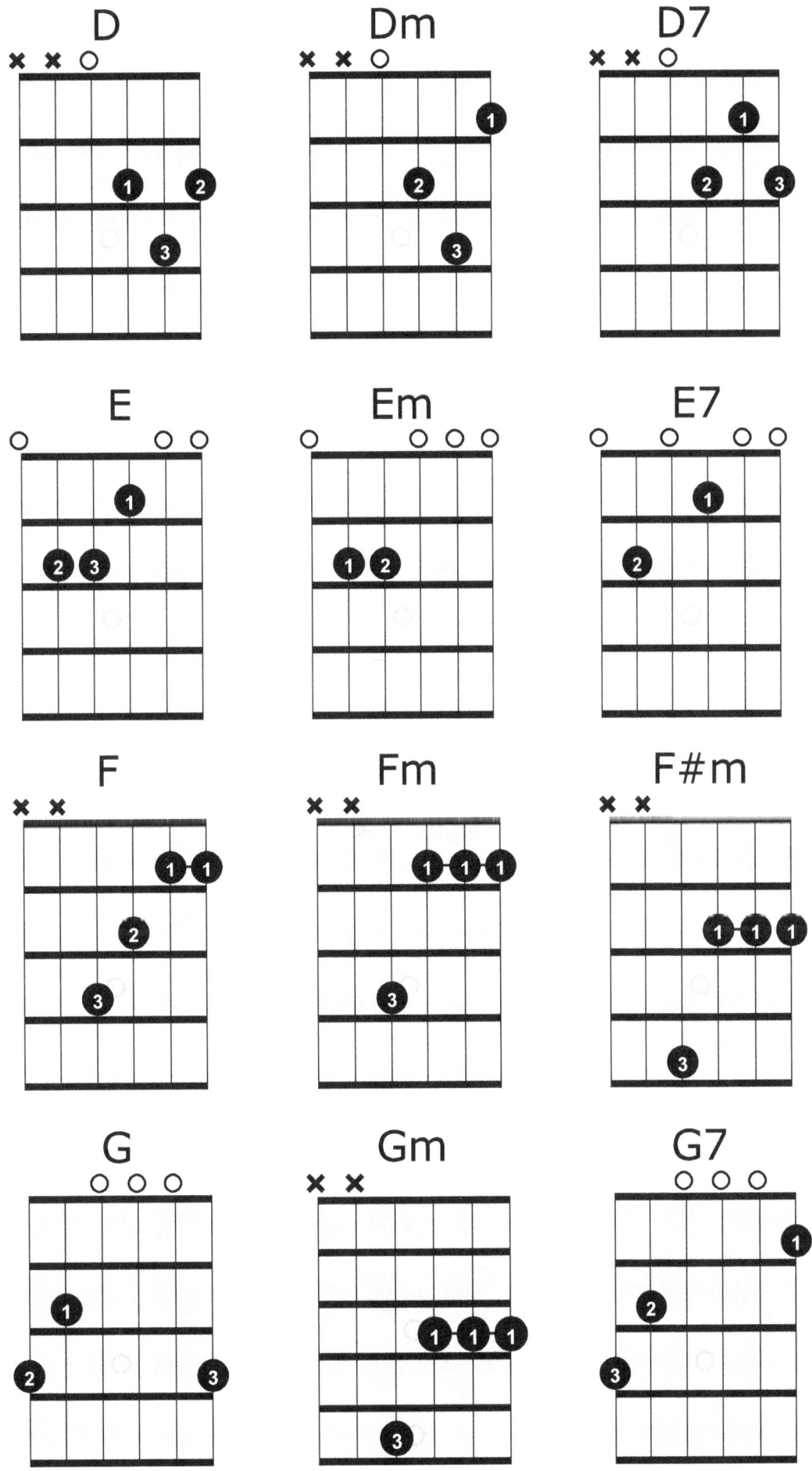

HOW TO USE A CAPO

A capo is a clamp that you place over your strings. It allows you to change keys quickly and use familiar chord shapes in different areas of the neck in order to get higher sounding chords.

Example:

If you place the capo on the third fret and the play a G chord shape, what you are actually playing is the B♭ chord. As such, capos can be useful for playing chords and keys that aren't always guitar friendly.

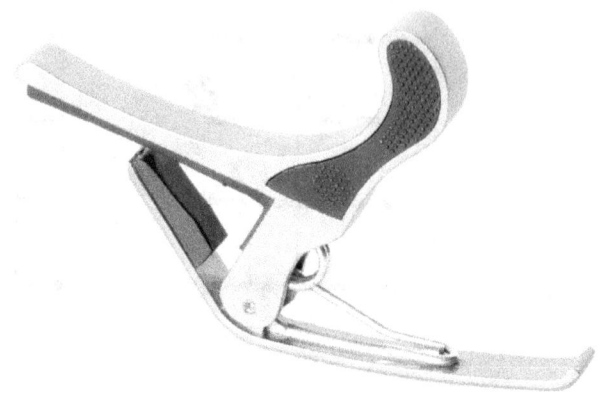

The Chord Shape	The Actual Sound
G	B♭

How it Works

Each fret marks a half step on the fretboard. Therefore, this capo on the third fret moves the notes up three half steps, and so the sound produced by the G chord shape is now a B♭ chord sound.

When you play barre chords (which we haven't really gotten into in this book, but you will likely come across in the future), your first finger acts like a capo, moving notes to higher pitches.

TRY IT: USING A CAPO

Place a capo on the third fret of your guitar. Then turn to the song, "Finding Peace," the Chord Practice Song found inside the Songs for Practice section. Now strum through the song. Note how the sound of each chord and the sound of the overall song have changed as a result. (If needed, remove the capo and play through it again so you can hear the difference.)

By adding the capo at the third fret, you have changed the **key** (the foundational sound) of the song. Now, instead of playing in the key of G (as you did without the capo), you are playing in the key of B♭.

Therefore, once the capo is placed on the third fret, the resulting chords for the song "Finding Peace" are: B♭, F, Gm, and E♭ for the verses, and E♭, F, Cm, and B♭ for the choruses. So it's the same song, same basic sound, with a new tonal center.

"FINDING PEACE" CHORD SOUND CHANGES

	Original Chords	New Chord Sounds
Verse	G D Em C	B♭ F Gm E♭
Chorus	Em D Am G C	Gm F Cm B♭ E♭

The capo can be placed anywhere on the neck, not just the third fret.
For more on capos and how to figure out what chord you are playing, check out *Guitar Chord Master 2: Beyond Basic Chords* from The Missing Method for Guitar..

HOW TO CHANGE YOUR GUITAR STRINGS

How often guitar strings need to be changed depends largely on how often you use them. However, every six months is a good general rule of thumb.

The first time I changed my strings I had no one to show me how to do it. I also had no books or videos to refer to. It was just me, a pack of new strings, a pair of old pliers, and a whole lot of frustration. That first time took me over three hours. Now, after years of practice, I can change an entire set of strings in about twenty minutes with no trouble (usually).

While every type of guitar is different, there are a few basic steps you'll want to take to make sure the string change goes smoothly. I recommend you read all the way through these instructions once before trying it and then again step by step as you change the strings on your guitar.

Step 1: Though you can remove all the strings and simply replace them, this is not recommended. It is best to keep some tension on the neck at all times. Therefore, it is often recommended to change the strings in sets of two. For example: first remove strings 6 and 3, then replace them; then remove strings 5 and 2, then replace them; finally, remove strings 4 and 1, then replace them. That way the tension on the neck remains fairly constant so that you won't have to make any neck adjustments after your new strings are on.

Using a string winder

Step 2: To remove an old string, unwind the string using the tuning keys. Next, remove the string peg at the bridge of the guitar. You may want to use a string winding tool to assist you with both of these tasks. The other end of the winder can be used to pry the string peg free.

Step 3: Once the old string is removed, you can then place the new string on. The first step is to place the new string in the bridge. On acoustic guitars, you place the ball end of the string into the peg-hole, then place the peg back in its place over the string (see photo on opposite page).

Step 4: Once the string is firmly in place in the bridge, your next step is to attach the string by winding it around the post on the headstock. To do this, first pull the string taught. Then you'll notice that you have way too much string to work with. What I do is cut the top of the string using wire cutters. *Be careful not to cut too much, otherwise you'll need to get a new set of strings and start over.* I usually cut about two to three inches depending on which string I'm putting on and how much slack I need.

Once the string is cut, feed the tip of the string through the hole in the post. Then bend the string around the post, tucking it under itself as you bend it around. Then hold your thumb over the nut to keep the string steady. This will help you wrap it around the post neatly. Use the winding tool (or your hand) to wind the string. Continue winding until it is tight. Do not over-wind. It could break the string.

Note: Make sure you take careful note as to what the strings look like before you remove them. You'll want to make sure you don't wind the wrong way around the post.

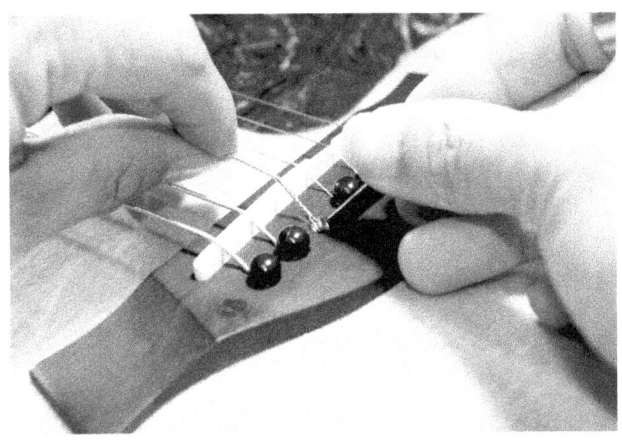

Place the ball end of the string into the peg-hole on acoustics.

Step 5: Once all the strings are in place, tune the guitar a half step higher than usual. This will stretch the strings and allow them to more quickly stabilize. Once all the strings are tuned high, go back and tune them to standard tuning.

Step 6: If you still have excess string hanging off the end, simply cut it off with wire cutters. While some people like the scraggly-wires look, they often end up getting in the way and can even scratch up the finish of your instrument.

Like everything, changing strings takes practice and gets easier each time you do it. If it's not perfect this time, don't sweat it. It was a learning experience and you'll be that much more prepared the next time around.

ABOUT THE AUTHOR

Christian Triola is a professional guitar teacher and author of over two dozen popular guitar method books, including The Missing Method for Guitar Note Reading Series and the Guitar Chord Master Series. His books arose out of a need for method books that didn't already exist for his students, so they address the needs real students have when learning guitar. With over 20 years of experience, he has taught thousands of students to learn guitar so they can play and create music they love. Christian holds a Master's Degree in Education and a Bachelor's Degree in Music (Jazz Studies), and has played in a variety of bands in addition to his many solo performances. When he's not teaching or playing guitar, he enjoys writing fiction and hiking the Cuyahoga Valley with his wife, Amy Joy. You can connect with him on social media and find all his books at TheMissingMethod.com.

What is The Missing Method?

We make it easy to learn guitar with books that focus on building one skill at a time. From the basics to chord and note reading mastery, we'll help you build the skills you need to play the music you love.

Find what you've been missing at TheMissingMethod.com.

www.ingramcontent.com/pod-product-compliance
Lightning Source LLC
Chambersburg PA
CBHW081458070526
44586CB00019B/2415